CONTENTS

Helion & Company Limited
Unit 8 Amherst Business Centre
Budbrooke Road
Warwick
CV34 5WE
England
Tel. 01926 499 619
Email: info@helion.co.uk
Website: www.helion.co.uk
Twitter: @helionbooks
https://helionbooks.wordpress.com/

Colour profiles and diagrams: Anderson Subtil

Cover photo: Polish Navy's Whiskey-class submarine Sokół at sea in 1978. (Photo via Stowarzyszenie Entuzjastow ORP Ślązak i Sympatykow Marynarki Wojennej)

Designed and typeset by Mach 3 Solutions (www.mach3solutions.co.uk)
Cover design Paul Hewitt, Battlefield Design (www.battlefield-design.co.uk)

ISBN: 978-1-804515-61-7

British Library Cataloguing-in-Publication Data
A catalogue record for this book is available from the British Library

We always welcome receiving book proposals from prospective authors.

Note: In order to simplify the use of this book, all names, locations and geographic designations are as provided in *The Times World Atlas*, or other traditionally accepted major sources of reference, as of the time of described events.

ABBREVIATIONS AND ACRONYMS

AShM	Anti-Ship missile
ASW	Anti-submarine warfare
DDR	*Deutsche Demokratische Republik* (German for German Democratic Republic; East Germany, 1947-1989)
DIVKASEL	Divisi Kapal Selam (Submarine Division)
DPRK	Democratic People's Republic of Korea
EON	*Экспедиции особого назначения* (Russian for '*Special Purpose Expedition*')
KRI	*Kapal Republik Indonesia* (Ship of the Republic of Indonesia)
MLU	Mid-Life Upgrade
NATO	North Atlantic Treaty Organisation
ORP	*Okręt Rzeczypospolitej Polskiej* (Ship of the Republic of Poland)
PLAN	People's Liberation Army Navy
PRC	People's Republic of China
RI	*Republik Indonesia*
SEKASAL	Sekolah Kapal Selam (The Submarine School)
SOF	Special Operations Forces
UAR	United Arab Republic (Union of Egypt and Syria, 1958-1961, and Egypt, 1961-1972)
USSR	Union of Soviet Socialist Republics

ACKNOWLEDGMENTS

The creation of the book would have been impossible without the use of the rich material on the history of the construction and service of Project 613 (*Whiskey*) submarines, contained in the books and publications of S.S. Berezhny, A.V. Batarshev, V.P. Zablotsky, A.A. Postnov and many other Russian/Soviet authors.

Among the most used foreign sources, in addition to the classic *Jane's Fighting Ships* and *Conway's All the World's Fighting Ships*, I would like to highlight the publications of such well-known authors and enthusiasts as Edgar O'Balance, Tadeusz Grzesikowski, and several others.

The most important sources of information and often very rare photographs were numerous Russian and foreign internet resources, especially specialised forums and blogs dedicated to naval topics. Among Russian Internet sources, this is primarily the site http://forums.airbase.ru (also known as 'Balancer Forums'), the book made extensive use of photographs, data and comments posted by respected participants of this resource. The author would like to say special thanks for the information to the brilliant researcher of the supply of Soviet naval equipment abroad, Alexander Rozin with his profound resource http://alerozin.narod.ru.

Among the foreign participants in forums devoted to naval topics, I would like to highlight: the Polish writer and researcher Krzysztof Dabrowski, who shared information about the career of Soviet submarines in Poland, the Japanese participant of the site https://forum.axishistory.com under the nickname *fontessa*, as well as the Indonesian member of the https://defencehub.live forum under the nickname *Gary*.

My special gratitude goes to the editor of the former acig.info website and forum, and editor of the six @War book-series, Tom Cooper who helped this book to go international.

Finally, I would like to thank my friends and colleagues for their support in writing the book, the subject of which does not intersect absolutely with the 'civilian' profession of the author, as well as my wife for help in preparing the book and, especially, for her patience and acceptance of the fact that several months of family life were spent on another book project.

INTRODUCTION

The first 10-years' shipbuilding programme of the Union of Soviet Socialist Republics (USSR; colloquially 'Soviet Union') after the Second World War, deserves a separate detailed book and has received, undeservedly, little attention in the publishing world, no matter where. A country that had just emerged from a devastating war, and had only 52 percent of its pre-war shipbuilding capacity, managed to put into mass production a number of classes of warships, the scale of production of which was never repeated again – regardless of whether in Soviet- or post-Soviet times. And, although Comrade Iosif Vissarionovich Stalin did not approve the construction of aircraft carriers and battleships, and 100 percent fulfilment of the programmes was not achieved in any class of ships, the number of produced cruisers of Project 68-bis (ASCC/NATO-reporting name: *Sverdlov*-class), destroyers of Project 30-bis (ASCC/NATO reporting name: *Skory*-class), patrol ships of Project 50 (ASCC/NATO reporting name: *Riga*-class), large submarine chasers of Project 122bis (ASCC/NATO reporting name: *Kronshtadt*-class), torpedo boats of Project 183 (ASCC/NATO reporting name: *Bolshevik*-class), minesweepers of Project 254 (ASCC/NATO reporting name: *T-43*-class), and other ships, is absolutely striking. The production of submarines provided even more reasons for amazement.

The Soviet leadership, obviously influenced by the successes of German submarines in the first half of the Second World War, decided to focus on the production of submarines, especially after receiving the latest captured German technologies. Obviously, the construction of 59 boats of the old pre-war *Shchuka*-, *Stalinets*- and *Malyutka*-classes was rather a quantitative indicator of the growth of the capabilities of the Soviet fleet, but the subsequent launch of modern post-war submarines into production was a colossal breakthrough for the Soviet Navy. And whilst production of Project-615 (ASCC/NATO reporting name: *Quebec*-class) submarines, with a revolutionary single engine operating in a closed cycle using oxygen to oxidise fuel and a solid chemical absorber to remove carbon dioxide (nowadays, such an engine would be called an 'air-independent propulsion'), turned out to be unsuccessful due to the unreliability of the power plant, then the production of other submarines based on the use of German technologies turned out to be very successful indeed. This applied to both large Project-611 submarines (ASCC/NATO reporting name: *Zulu*-class), and, especially, the Project-613 conventionally powered attack submarines (ASCC/NATO reporting name: *Whiskey*-class).

The purpose of the book is not to consider the history of the development and production of Project 613 submarines, or its performance characteristics and numerous modifications. There are dozens of Russian and foreign editions and publications on these topics. It is sufficient to briefly note that the design of the submarines of this project became possible after Soviet scientists and design bureaus received access to captured German submarines of Type VII and Type XXI, which contained a number of revolutionary innovations. 'Creative borrowing', coupled with their own modifications, made it possible to create the most widespread diesel submarine that was ever produced after the Second World War. A total of 215 submarines were built in the USSR, of which 113 in the city of Gorky (nowadays Nizhny Novgorod), at plant No.112; 72 in the city of Nikolaev (nowadays Mykolaiv, in Ukraine), at plant No.444; 19 in the city of Leningrad (nowadays Saint Petersburg), at plant No.189, and 11 in Komsomolsk-on-Amur, at plant No.199. Also, 21 submarines of this project were launched from the stocks of two Chinese shipyards in the late 1950s and early 1960s. In the West, according to ASCC/NATO classification, these submarines received the designation *Whiskey*-class and it is under this name that this project is known worldwide – even more so because submarines of this type travelled far from their native shores, exploring the North Atlantic, the North Pacific Ocean, and for the first time 'penetrating' the Mediterranean Sea.

The saturation of the Soviet Navy with submarines of this project, the launch of more modern submarines of Project 633 (ASCC/NATO reporting name: *Romeo*-class) and Project 641 (ASCC/NATO reporting name: *Foxtrot*-class) into production, and the start of production of nuclear submarines, allowed the Soviet Union to allocate a significant number of submarines of Project 613 for transfer to allies and friendly countries.

That said, *Whiskeys* were not the first submarines that the USSR supplied abroad. In the early 1950s, several allied countries (including the People's Republic of China (PRC), Poland, and Bulgaria) received submarines of *Stalinets*- and *Malyutka*-classes: these were pre-war designs, of course, and could not pose any serious threat to the fleets of countries hostile to the socialist camp. Only the supply of *Whiskey* submarines allowed countries friendly to the USSR to receive combat submarines that were truly dangerous for the enemy. In modern Western publications one can find somewhat condescending notes in relation to the submarines of this project, which are described as submarines with a rather coastal range, increased noise and, basically, of low danger for the numerous anti-submarine ships of NATO countries. However, it was the service of these submarines in foreign navies that made it possible to partially dispel these prejudices, and the author sees one of his tasks as demonstrating the positive foreign experience of using *Whiskeys*. The main objective of the book is to acquaint, the general reader with the little-studied topics of the service of *Whiskey* submarines in foreign navies, to share information about little-known or generally unknown events and incidents during the service of these boats outside the USSR, and also to introduce the biographies of a number of the submarines' commanders from different foreign fleets.

Looking ahead, we note that submarines of this class participated in several wars and armed conflicts, did not suffer losses, but could neither boast of victories. However, their main merit lay in something else: the fleet of each country that received *Whiskeys* for service immediately moved to a 'higher league' of maritime powers, causing fear among potential enemies. We will see in the book, taking the example of Indonesia, how seriously the aggressive and regular use of Project 613 submarines made it possible to strengthen the political weight of the country. For a number of countries, the *Whiskey*-class became the first submarine in the histories of their fleets. For China this project became particularly noteworthy, as it was the first submarine in the history of the Chinese shipbuilding industry to be put into production. *Whiskey* diesel submarines were one of the most important tools for strengthening Soviet allies and satellites, as well as being a demonstrator of the capabilities of Soviet industry.

1

ALBANIAN WHISKEYS

Perhaps the most unusual operator of Project 613 submarines was Albania, which actively operated vessels of this class for about 30 years. In order to understand the reasons for the appearance of submarines in this country, it is necessary to delve a little into history. During the Second World War, the country was first occupied by the Italians and then by the Germans. Unlike most Eastern European countries, Albanian partisans, whose ranks numbered 70,000 people (out of a country's population of 1.1 million people), independently liberated their state. In the conditions of an underdeveloped agrarian country, when other political forces were discredited by cooperation with the occupiers, the Albanian communists won the post-war struggle for power: in the elections to the People's Assembly of Albania of December 1945, the communist-controlled Democratic Front received 93% of the votes. The resulting government was headed by the first secretary of the Albanian Communist Party, Enver Hoxha. In March 1946 Albania was proclaimed a People's Republic. Hoxha declared himself a convinced Marxist-Leninist and admired the personality of Stalin. Stalin had already announced his support for the new Albania during Hoxha's visit to the USSR in June 1945. Hoxha was present at the Victory Parade, visited Stalingrad, and received assurances of Soviet technical and scientific assistance. In the summer of 1947, Hoxha returned to the USSR. Stalin presented him with the Order of Suvorov, which Enver always wore during official ceremonies. Albania was provided with a preferential loan

I.V. Stalin, V.M. Molotov, E. Hoxha (far right) on the podium of the Mausoleum, Moscow, 7 November 1947. (Photo via www.artofwar.ru)

for the purchase of various goods. Hoxha said at a Kremlin dinner that: 'Stalin and the Soviet Union are our saviours and comrades. We Albanians pledge eternal friendship and devotion to you.'

Under Stalin, the Soviet Union began to provide significant economic and military assistance to Albania, and the country began to receive large volumes of Soviet weapons, although it was still far from receiving submarines.

It is worth noting that, starting from the late 1940s, Albania existed in a hostile environment. This was due to the political conflict with the Socialist Federative Republic of Yugoslavia, because Hoxha supported Stalin's position in the conflict with the Yugoslav leader Josip Broz 'Tito', and the near military confrontations with Italy and Greece, which joined NATO in 1949 and 1952 respectively. Moreover, in August 1949, the Albanian army participated in a military conflict in the Albanian-Greek borderland, supporting rebel Greek communists.

The Soviet-Albanian idyll did not last long. Ideological disagreements began in 1954-55, due to the rapprochement between the USSR and Yugoslavia, but especially intensified after the famous 20th Congress of the Communist Party of the Soviet Union, which led to the debunking of the cult of Stalin and the revision of Stalinist practices in foreign and domestic policy in the Soviet Union. The Albanian leadership, led by E. Hoxha, did not follow Khrushchev's new course, despite the continuation of very close Soviet-Albanian economic and military-technical relations. At the end of 1956, an attempt by part of the Albanian communist party elite to displace E. Hoxha and his close associates, and to follow new Soviet realities, failed, after which the leaders of the 'opposition' were demonstrably repressed.

In 1957, E. Hoxha tried to improve relations with Moscow: he proposed the establishment of a Soviet Navy base in Albania, in the Pasha Liman Bay of the Gulf of Vlora. The offer was attractive: warships of the Soviet Union were able to anchor 70 kilometres off the coast of Italy, and submarines with ballistic missiles could cover the whole of Europe in a single salvo. The USSR willingly agreed with the idea of creating such a bridgehead 'under the nose' of NATO; it was in the process of creating this base and to provide this base with protection that the Albanians received relatively modern warships, which formed the backbone of the fleet for the entire subsequent period of communist Albania.

According to Albanian sources, the Soviet proposal to create a logistics point for Soviet ships in Albania was discussed for the first time during the visit of the Albanian military-governmental delegation to Moscow in early February 1957; the Albanian Minister of Defence Bekir Baluku (Albanian: Beqir Balluku) participated in the negotiations on this issue with the commander of the Allied Forces of the Warsaw Pact countries, Marshal Konev, and deputy commander of the Soviet Navy, Admiral Fokin. The day after Baluku returned home, the Albanian leadership agreed to conclude an agreement on the creation of a joint Albanian-Soviet naval base in Albania. To prepare the agreement, Albanian and Soviet working groups were created, which were headed by the Chief of the Albanian General Staff, General Arif Hasko and Deputy Commander of the Black Sea Fleet, Vice Admiral S.E. Chursin.

As a result of their work, in Tirana, on 12 September 1957, General Arif Hasko and Admiral Fokin signed the first agreement on the establishment of a naval base in the Gulf of Vlora, which provided for the development of coastal infrastructure in the bay for the deployment of submarines and support ships.

At the same time, in the autumn of 1957, the commander of the Black Sea Fleet A.V. Kasatonov introduced to the Commander-in-Chief of the Soviet Navy S.G. Gorshkov proposals for the use of Albania for basing the Soviet Navy in the Mediterranean. It was proposed to place 10-12 submarines in the Pasha Liman Bay of the Gulf of Vlora, to use a division of anti-submarine ships and anti-submarine helicopters to defend the base, and also to transfer to the Albanians four divisions of shore-based P-1 Strela anti-ship missiles (NATO reporting name: *SS-N-1 Scrubber*). In addition, it was planned to base an air regiment of Tu-16 bombers (NATO reporting name: *Badger*) at the Albanian airfield.

In October 1957, the Soviet Minister of Defence Marshal G.K. Zhukov visited Albania on the project 68-K cruiser *Kuibyshev* (NATO reporting name: *Chapayev*-class). Among other things, Zhukov visited Vlora, and then inspected the southwestern part of the Gulf of Vlora, in the area of the Ravenes plateau of the Karaburun Peninsula, as construction of the main facilities of the submarine base had already begun in Pasha Liman Bay at the time of his visit.

In general, the history of the creation of the Soviet naval base is well described in publishing, so we will focus on the issue of the appearance of submarines in Albania. Of the 12 submarines planned for deployment at Pasha Liman, several were to be equipped with Albanian crews trained by their Soviet comrades.

By the last days of November 1957, the First Submarine Brigade was formed in Albania. The first speaker at the ceremony was General Nexhip Vilçani, then Commander of the Coastal Defence, who briefly spoke about the importance of the newly formed brigade and its role in enhancing the country's defence capabilities. Following this, the commander of the Naval Combat Fleet, Admiral Abdi Mati, read out the order of the Minister of Defence on the creation of a submarine brigade and the list of names of the unit's command staff, along with the submarine crews. Thus, Captain 2nd Rank Djemal Shani was appointed as commander of the submarine brigade, Commander Dashamir Ohri was appointed as a commander of the first submarine, Commander Muharrem Lulolli took the second, commander Spiro Kote the third, and, lastly, commander Shyqyri Çukaj was appointed to command the fourth submarine.[1]

To equip future Albanian submarines, Albanian personnel were carefully selected for service in this formation, they arrived first in Odessa on a sea liner, and then by military transport went to Sevastopol, where they underwent five months of training. Submarine crews were formed from Albanians, and training of officers and sailors was carried out both individually and immediately as part of the crews. In total, during 1958-59, 307 Albanian submariners were trained in the Sevastopol 11th training detachment.

In the summer of 1958, the first group of four *Whiskey* diesel-electric submarines and the depot ship *Vladimir Nemchinov* entered the Vlora Bay of the Adriatic Sea, and later eight more submarines arrived. So, under the noses of its enemies, the USSR formed the 40th separate submarine division under the command of Rear Admiral Georgy Yegorov.

The story of the transition from the Baltic to the Albanian port of 4 submarines (*S-241*, *S-242*, *S-358* and *S-360*) and depot ship *Vladimir Nemchinov* deserves a separate description. On 1 August 1958 (according to Soviet data, on 4 August), four submarines, a depot ship and a tanker set off from the port of Baltiysk. The small Albanian accompanying group included the aforementioned submarine brigade commander Djemal Shani and the four future submarine commanders who were on the submarines. Abeam the English port of Dover, the tanker refuelled the submarines and returned to the Baltic. In the Bay of Biscay, the ships were caught in a strong storm, and while the submerged submarines survived the violence of the sea without problems, the depot ship was seriously battered. However, the ships successfully reached Gibraltar, and while in the Mediterranean the journey to Albania took place in almost ideal conditions. The submarines and depot ship reached the Gulf of Vlora on 21 August.

After reaching Albania, in addition to the Soviet crew, each of the submarines was assigned an Albanian backup crew and from September 1958 the implementation of the training plan for Albanian crews, who arrived from their initial Sevastopol deployment, began. To support the basing of submarines, a Soviet floating dock arrived in Pasha Liman in 1958. Despite the presence of Albanian backup crews, these 4 submarines were operated mainly by Soviet sailors. For example, from November-December 1959, submarine *S-360*, under the command of Captain V.S. Kozlov, from Pasha Liman Bay made her first trip towards Gibraltar and back completely underwater. During this voyage, the submarine whilst in the Strait of Tunisia discovered a detachment of American ships led by the cruiser *Des Moines*, on which American President Eisenhower was returning to the United States. According to Albanian sources, only four Albanian sailors were on board of *S-360*, including Şüküri Cukaj, the commander of the corresponding Albanian backup crew. Perhaps, at that moment, the Soviet instructors did not trust their Albanian comrades with long underwater crossings.

Parallel with the improvement in interaction between the Navies of the two countries, however, political relations between the USSR and Albania continued to deteriorate. On 25 May 1959, General Secretary N.S. Khrushchev arrived in Tirana by Tu-104 plane on an official visit, he was accompanied by the Minister of Defence of the USSR R. Malinovsky, Deputy Minister of Foreign

Albanian naval officer Dashamir Ohri, first commander of one of the four submarines of the Albanian Navy, and future commander of the Submarine Brigade. (via Albanian Internet)

Affairs N.P. Firyubin (former Soviet ambassador to Belgrade during the reconciliation between Khrushchev and Tito). In the ongoing campaign to expose Stalin's cult of personality, Khrushchev encountered the reluctance of a number of communist leaders to follow his path. With the intention of conveying his position to the Albanian leader E. Hoxha, he flew to Albania; in addition, he wanted to personally verify the state of affairs in the country. Khrushchev had big plans for Albania; he wanted to install Soviet missiles here as a counterweight to the American missiles deployed in Italy: '...if medium-range missiles or even short-range missiles are installed in Albania, they can cover the whole of Italy.'

However, despite the warm welcome, Khrushchev behaved unreasonably during this visit. He demanded that Hoxha change his policy and threatened to stop the supply of Soviet goods and weapons.

The turning point occurred in 1960. First, at a meeting in Bucharest, representatives of Albania flatly refused to condemn the mistakes of the Chinese Communist Party, and a few months later in Moscow, Enver Hoxha stated that the USSR's course towards peaceful coexistence with the West was wrong and only a world revolution could eliminate the threat of nuclear war.

It is interesting that despite the disagreements that arose between the leaders of the USSR and Albania, relations between sailors in 1960 continued to remain positive. As Rear Admiral Zagrebin recalled, 'throughout 1960 our military, in particular sailors, worked very friendly with the Albanians, there were no conflicts.' The port

N.S. Khrushchev and E. Hoxha at the naval base in Pasha Liman Bay, surrounded by Soviet and Albanian sailors, May 1959. (via Albanian Internet)

in Durres was expanded, military facilities were built in the Gulf of Vlora for basing ships and anti-landing defence of the coast. At the end of 1960, Soviet 40th separate submarine brigade transferred, as was previously agreed, 4 submarines *S-241*, *S-242*, *S-358*, *S-360* and depot ship *Vladimir Nemchinov* to the Albanian fleet. The handover ceremony in the Gulf of Vlora, which took place very solemnly, was attended by the leaders of the Albanian fleet and officers of the General Staff of the Albanian Armed Forces. But even after the transfer of the boats, at the request of the Albanians, Russian officers and foremen continued to train the Albanians and go to sea with them. The loading and manoeuvring of the boats took place under the direct supervision of Soviet officers.[2]

But, by at the beginning of 1961, the situation at the naval base deteriorated sharply. The Albanians created unbearable conditions for Soviet sailors; the base practically lost its combat effectiveness. It became apparent that the Albanians considered all the ships at the base in Vlora to be their property. Allegedly, the USSR had promised under the agreement to transfer all 12 submarines and auxiliary vessels to Albania.

'The Vlora base has become a bone of contention,' wrote Enver Hoxha in his book *Khrushchevites*.

> There was no doubt that the base was ours. We could never agree that even an inch of our land should be under the heel of foreigners. According to an official, clearly formulated and signed by both governments' agreement, in which there was no room for any ambiguity, the Vlora base belonged to Albania and at the same time was supposed to serve the defense of the socialist camp. The Soviet Union, the agreement stated, must provide 12 submarines and several auxiliary vessels.

There was really something big to profit from at the base: in addition to 12 submarines and a depot ship in Vlora there was a radio-technical reconnaissance ship *Ugor*, a reconnaissance ship *Crab*, and on the island of Sazan there were a brigade of guard ships with a division of minesweepers. According to the memoirs from the Soviet side, the Albanians behaved disgracefully: they damaged property, argued with Soviet sailors every day – provoking them into fights and quarrels –, and literally shit on the porch of the commandant's office.

At a meeting in Moscow on 28-29 March 1961, Albanian Defence Minister Bekir Baluku refused to transfer the base to Soviet control, after which Soviet Defence Minister A.A. Grechko began to insist on transferring the base to the Command of the United Armed Forces of the Warsaw Pact countries. However, the Albanians refused this form of continuing Soviet military presence in Albania. The principal problem was to determine the fate of the ships and base

Cover of Enver Hoxha's famous book *The Khrushvhevites*. (via Albanian internet)

infrastructure. On 25 April 1961, the Albanian leadership stated that it had no objections to an option for dividing the naval personnel of the base, by which the USSR would retain those naval assets serviced by Soviet crews. The Soviet delegation led by Deputy Minister of Foreign Affairs N.P. Firyubin took part in further negotiations with the participation of the Chief of Staff of the Allied Forces of the Warsaw Pact, General A.I. Antonov, and the commander of the Black Sea Fleet, Admiral Kasatonov, who ultimately accepted the Albanians' proposal to divide the ships at the base in the Gulf of Vlora, and the withdrawal of the Soviet assigned ships along with all Soviet crews and Soviet base personnel.

To return the Soviet submarines with their crews home, the commander of the Black Sea Fleet, Admiral Igor Kasatonov, arrived in Albania on Project 57-bis destroyer *Uporny* (NATO reporting name: *Krupny*-class). However, this was not easy to do. The Albanians declared that four of the 12 submarines belonged to them and refused to return them to the USSR. Admiral Kasatonov managed to withdraw from Pasha Liman Bay only the floating submarine base, *Viktor Kotelnikov* and eight submarines, which had exclusively Soviet crews. As a result, on 26 May 1961, eight submarines, *Viktor Kotelnikov*, a headquarters ship, a floating dock and a number of other auxiliary ships with Soviet crews and base personnel left the Gulf of Vlora and set off for the Baltic Sea. This ended the Soviet military presence in Albania.

In addition to the submarines, the Albanians took command of five torpedo boats of Project 123-bis (NATO reporting name: *Komsomolets*-class), four anti-submarine chasers of Project 122 (BO-2 type), eight minesweepers, a demagnetisation vessel, two tankers, a torpedo-recovery boat of Project 368T, a diving boat, a tugboat, 11 fast boats and a floating dock. As Russian sources run, the USSR literally 'gifted' an entire fleet to the Albanians. When the Soviet sailors left, the Albanians saw them off with the muzzles of guns from the former Soviet ships. 'The admiral was forced to take only the submarines served by Soviet crews, and, with his tail between his legs, leave the bay and go home,' wrote the Albanian leader.[3]

Nikita Khrushchev never decided to fundamentally deal with tiny Albania: he was afraid of a military conflict with the People's Republic of China. 'They're crazy!' is how he described the Albanian leaders. 'We will recall all specialists, including those who are still there. We took away eight submarines, the Albanians captured four submarines, which had a mixed Soviet-Albanian command. This is naive piracy. Not to mention the fact that these are outdated submarines, the Albanians will soon run out of spare parts – even if we leave them with them.'[4]

Soviet ships leave Albania forever. (via 'Detaria Shqiptare ne Rrjedhen e Kohes', 2018)

Here the author must make a small digression and comment on the words of Soviet and Russian sources about the 'piracy' of the Albanian side. It is quite plausible that a number of surface ships were captured illegally, but the four submarines that the Albanians got (the former *S-241*, *S-242*, *S-358* and *S-360*) were specifically intended for the Navy of Albania and the Soviet side prepared crews from local officers and sailors for them. Moreover, the boats were actually transferred to Albania at the end of 1960. Obviously, at the peak of tension, both sides behaved incorrectly; for example, according to Albanian data, Soviet officers tried to take away one

Four *Whiskeys* already as a part of the Albanian Navy. (via artofwar.ru)

of the four submarines intended for Albania. In turn, in the spring of 1961, the Albanians refused to provide Soviet sailors with spare parts for Soviet submarines, which were supplied and stored in Albania by the Soviet side for all 12 Project 613 submarines based in Pasha Liman. Naturally, Albania did not pay anything for the import of weapons, but no one expected that the poorest country in Europe will be able to pay for large-scale Soviet supplies. The Albanians, to some extent, rightly noted that they paid with the possibility of basing in the Mediterranean.

At the same time, some accusations from the Albanian side reached the point of absurdity. For example, one of the most famous submariners of Albania of the 1960s and 1970s, Jak Mandrea, in an interview from 2014 seriously claimed that the Russians (as Albanians describe Soviet sailors in modern publications) seriously damaged three submarines at the base in Pasha Liman. Allegedly, they perforated their main hull, which meant that the submarines could not withstand the pressure of water at depths of more than 30 metres. The body of the submarine was made of special metal and could withstand immersion to a depth of 180 metres. But Soviet officers apparently had poured a dangerous liquid (acid) into three submarines, which 'ate through' their hulls. When Soviet officers left Albania, they warned their Albanian colleagues: 'be careful, you will drown!' The warning was seemingly taken at face value, as the commander of the fleet, Admiral Avdi Mati, ordered that under no circumstances should the boats dive more than 30 metres deep. Jak Mandrea was the commander of one of the submarines at the time, and he reported that the damage was repaired only with the help of Chinese specialists.[5] Obviously, even 50 years after the rupture of relations between the two countries, paranoid sentiments towards the Soviet revisionists are still alive among the older generation of Albanians. In fairness, we note that in other Albanian studies on the topic, damage to the boats is explained by the natural causes.

As a result of the political machinations, the relations between Moscow and Tirana were severed in December 1961. Khrushchev tried to establish them again – in 1963 – but the Albanians flatly refused to cooperate. They were proud of the capture of Soviet submarines for a long time; for them this incident became part of a heroic epic: in 1979 they even made the feature film *Face to Face*, which showed the incident with submarines in the spirit of the confrontation between 'true Marxists-Leninists' and 'Khrushchevites'. Of course, the Albanians were presented in it as real 'Leninists' and the Soviet sailors were presented as evil and vile 'Khrushchevites'. Unsurprisingly, we will return to this film later on.

As part of the Albanian Navy, the newly acquired submarines received the following designations:

- *S-241* = *Stuhia*,
- *S-242* = *Tufani*,
- *S-358* = *Rrufeja*, and
- *S-360* = *Vetëtima*.

These boats were often designated in Albanian sources as *ND-1*, *ND-2*, *ND-3*, *ND-4*, respectively. It is important to note that even in Albanian publications there is great confusion with the names of the submarines, not to mention the dozens of different pennant numbers that were assigned to the boats during their service in the Albanian fleet. Unfortunately, even former submarine commanders often, many years after completing their service in the navy, invented non-existent stories about the service of Albanian submarines, therefore, any research on the Albanian fleet is and will be fraught with inaccuracies and guesswork (it also applies to this book).

Perhaps the Soviet leaders and military leadership expected that the Albanian Navy would have difficulty maintaining Soviet naval equipment in combat-ready condition, which seemed quite reasonable. But the Albanian leadership found an elegant solution to this problem with the help of their Chinese comrades. Also, the Chinese leadership, having quarrelled excessively with Khrushchev, was not slow to come to the aid of Albania. In return, Albania began to support Chinese interests in the UN. The Albanian leadership skilfully played on the Sino-Soviet contradictions, supporting the Chinese line of struggle against the Soviet revisionists. The history of cooperation between Albania and Maoist China deserves a separate study; we only note that the Chinese comrades repeated Soviet mistakes, supplying almost one and a half billion yuan worth of weapons to Albania for free, including more than a hundred jet fighters, more than 800 tanks and armoured vehicles, thousands of guns, dozens of torpedoes and patrol boats, helicopters, anti-aircraft missiles, and helped Albania to master the production of Kalashnikov assault rifles (by post-communist times, Albanian-made AKs were actively sold to all hot spots of the world). But we are primarily interested in the help of Chinese comrades in maintaining submarines in combat readiness. The PRC, which had mastered the production of Project 613 submarines, had also accumulated significant experience in operating these ships. During the visit of the Albanian military delegation led by Bekir Baluku to China in 1964, naval issues were also considered. China undertook to build a ship repair plant in Albania and provide assistance in the repair of Albanian *Whiskeys*. Soon, 127 Chinese specialists in submarine technology and weapons arrived at the base in Pasha Liman, and they carried out work to restore the technical condition of four Albanian submarines in the period from 1965 to 1969.[6] In 1965, construction of a ship repair plant (Kantierit tK Riparimit tK Anijeve – K.R.A.F) began in Pasha Liman, which was carried out under the leadership and with the help of Chinese engineers and specialists. Thanks to Chinese assistance, technology and equipment (in particular, a 16-ton crane arrived from China), the ship repair plant was put into operation on 29 May 1969, and then existed as a separate military unit with the symbol of military unit 9093. With the construction of this plant, it became possible to carry out ship repair works on all types of ships and vessels of the Albanian fleet.[7]

It is worth noting that within 5 months after the departure of the Soviet ships, Albanian submarines began actively patrolling the country's coast, without, however, moving too far into the depths of the sea. Only after the repair and modernisation of the boats by Chinese specialists (completed by 1969), it should be noted, did Albanian submarines begin to go on expeditions to the Ionian and Mediterranean Seas.

In the meantime, while the Chinese comrades were building coastal infrastructure and repairing submarines, military ranks were abolished in 1966 in the Albanian armed forces and political commissars were restored. The submarine brigade was led by the brigade commander, Mark Plani and Commissar Dhori Jorgji.

- *ND-1*: Commander Aleko Pojani and Commissar Enver Kalluci
- *ND-2*: Commander Jak Mandrea and Commissar Skënder Doçi
- *ND-3*: Commander Petrit Myftiu and Commissar Ligor Thomai
- *ND-4*: Commander Ibrahim Juba and Commissar Beqir Gërbi

One of the first 'long-distance' trips of the Albanian Navy took place in September 1968, when two submarines entered the Ionian Sea to track NATO ships. While on the surface, the Albanian *Whiskeys* were tracked by an American warship and were overflown by many of NATO aircraft. In this situation, both submarines dived to periscope depth and headed for the Gulf of Taranto. Two Italian destroyers headed towards the Albanians, while three Albanian torpedo boats on the island of Sazan were in full combat readiness, awaiting the order to go to help the submarines. In the area of Cape Santa Maria di Leuca, the Albanian submarines turned around and went back to their base in Pasha Liman. This sortie of Albanian submarines served as a demonstration of the readiness of the Albanian Navy.[8]

In the 1970s, there were at least two expeditions of Albanian submarines far beyond the country's territorial waters in the submerged position: one along the route Albania-Malta-Peloponnese (in Greece)-Albania, the second – a 5-day stay in the waters of the Ionian Sea. Returning, the submarines helped the anti-submarine forces of the Albanian Navy practice technologies for countering the invasion of enemy submarine forces, simulating the submarines of a possible enemy. Also, training landings of naval SOF were carried out from Albanian submarines.

It is worth noting that as relations with China cooled in the second half of the 70s, certain difficulties began to arise with maintaining all the submarines in combat-ready condition. According to unconfirmed reports from *Jane's Fighting Ships*, *Tufani* (*ND-2*) submarine was withdrawn from the fleet. A possible cause being the cannibalisation of spare parts or an incident.

Towards the end of their career in the Albanian Navy, the submarines were transferred in 1987 to a new location – to a special underwater bunker for submarines in the bay of Porto Palermo in southern Albania. For the Albanians, who built a record number of bunkers per capita during the reign of Enver Hoxha (173 thousand bunkers in total), it was logical to build a well-protected bunker for submarines. Construction began in 1969 (according to other sources, in 1970). It is interesting that initially the bunker-tunnel in Porto Palermo rock masses was built to house missile boats, the delivery of which was expected from China. The work was carried out with the help of Chinese specialists and fortification battalions specially created for this purpose. In Porto Palermo, such a battalion, after its personnel exceeded 1,000 people, was reorganised in 1974-75 to the fortification regiment. The shelter had to withstand the impact of weapons of mass destruction.

However, the cooling of Albanian-Chinese relations, and then their rupture in 1978, put an end to the Albanian plans to obtain missile boats. It was then the Albanian Prime Minister and Minister of Defence Mehmet Shehu simultaneously proposed to reconstruct the facility in Porto Palermo for basing Albanian submarines. To do this, it turned out to be necessary to expand and deepen the tunnel-pool to a water depth of 7.5 metres (the original project provided for a water depth of 4.5 metres). Construction work in Porto Palermo continued and was completed only in the second half of the 1980s. As a result, a tunnel was built more than 650 metres long and 12 metres high, the entrance and exit to which was closed by a 32-ton gate.

For eight months – from June 1986 to March 1987 – tests for basing submarines were carried out in Porto Palermo. After this, in October 1987, a brigade of submarines from Pasha Liman was transferred to Porto Palermo, where three submarines were subsequently based (the fourth submarine docked at Pasha Liman in 1988 for repairs, which lasted eight years, but were never completed). This may have been the same *Tufani* that *Jane's Fighting Ships* 'decommissioned' in 1976. In their place, a naval group with torpedo boats from Sazan Island was relocated to Pasha Liman in 1988.[9]

The commander of the submarine brigade at that time was Dervish Jaupin, commissar Petrit Agon and chief of staff Vladimir Barjamin.

In 1992, the submarine brigade from Porto Palermo was again relocated to Pasha Liman.

In general, the combat readiness of the submarines was maintained for 33 years after the break with the USSR – until 1995.

After the fall of the communist regime in 1991 and the effective financial bankruptcy of Albania in the 1990s, the submarines were withdrawn from the active fleet. During the riots in January-March 1997, the naval base was looted, and even weapons, diesel engines and sailors' bunks were taken away from all vessels.[10]

After that, the submarines rusted in the port for another 13 years, until in 2010 it was decided to sell them (with the exception of one) for scrap metal. By this time, one of the boats had already sunk at the pier.[11]

View of the so-called 'Porto Palermo Tunnel' built for the Albanian *Whiskeys*. It was abandoned in 1998. (via Karel Jakubec)

Entrance to the abandoned bunker – submarine tunnel in Porto Palermo. (via www.outono.net)

Inside of the abandoned bunker – submarine tunnel in Porto Palermo. (via www.outono.net)

Albanian *Whiskeys* rusting in Pasha Liman in early 2000's (from left to right): *Tufani*, *Rrufeja*, *Vetetima* and *Stuhia* (painted in white). (Author's collection)

As a result, three of the four submarines were dismantled and melted down at a metallurgical plant in the city of Elbasan (Albania), and the fourth remained at the Pasha Liman naval base in order to be turned into a floating museum.[12] As already mentioned, in 1979, a grandiose (by Albanian standards) feature film *Face to Face* (Albanian: *Balle per Balle*) was shot, which shows one of the most difficult periods in the history of modern Albania – the break in Albanian-Soviet relations at the end of 1961. The central point of the film is the confrontation between Soviet and Albanian sailors in Pasha Liman in 1961. The film shows an Albanian submarine with pennant number 105, which Soviet sailors try to capture from the Albanians. Accordingly, it was decided to preserve the remaining fourth submarine as the main exhibit of the Cold War Museum with pennant number 105. The film was based on the novel by the most famous Albanian writer Ismail Kadare *The Winter of the Great Solitude* (Albanian: *Dimri i vetmisë së madhe*).

Still from the film *Face to Face*. (via www.medialb.com)

1. Nëndetsja e I[rë] nr. 305 STUHIA

Komandant	Kapiten i rangut të III[të] Dashamir Ohri
Zv.komandant	Kapiten Lejtenant I Paskal Thanasi
Zv.komandant për punë politike	Kapiten Selim Pira
Kryemekanik	Toger Ilmi Kapo

2. Nëndetsja e II[të] nr. 315 TUFANI

Komandant	Kapiten i parë Muharrem LLullolli
Zv.komandant	Toger Shezai Kasa
Zv.komandant për punë politike	Kapiten Enver Kalluçi
Kryemekanik	Toger Korab Mejdani

3. Nëndetsja e III[të] nr. 325 RRUFEJA

Komandant	Kapiten Lejtenant I[rë] Spiro Kote
Zv.komandant	Toger Resmi Shametaj
Zv.komandant për punë politike	Kapiten Mihal Zhamo
Kryemekanik	Toger Safet Hysi

4. Nëndetsja e IV[të] nr. 335 VETËTIMA

Komandant	Toger Shyqyri Çukaj
Zv.komandant	Toger Petrit Myftiu
Zv.komandant për punë politike	Kapiten Petrit Shehu
Kryemekanik	Toger Asti Popa

This photograph of the Albanian *Whiskeys* is complemented by a text with the names of the first commanders and senior officers of the Albanian submarines. (via www.balancer.ru)

The author has come across three versions about which of the four Albanian submarines remained as a museum, and cannot 100% confirm any one of them. It would seem that the photograph right should give a comprehensive answer that this was *Rrufeja*, but the problem is that the accompanying text says that *Rrufeja* (former *S-358*, built by the Baltic Shipyard, shipyard No.189 named after S. Ordzhonikidze in the city Leningrad) was built in the city of Gorky (a hint at the shipbuilding plant No.112 *Krasnoe Sormovo*, named after A.A. Zhdanov). This immediately undermines the credibility of the photograph. The author is inclined to believe that the most famous Albanian submarine *Stuhia* (formerly *S-241*), painted in white in the early 2000s, was installed as a museum exhibit and there are many references confirming this.[13] An alternative version is that the museum exhibit is the former *Tufani/S-242*, which was considered to be in the worst condition among Albanian submarines.

During its existence the Submarine Brigade was headed by the following commanders: Djemal Shani, Dashamir Ohri, Mark Plani, Petrit Muftiu, Fitim Halili, Aleko Pojani, Dervish Jaupin, Mit'hat Islami, and Bashkim Kryeziu.

Djemal Shani – the first commander of the Submarine Brigade – was born in 1927 into a poor family in the suburbs of Durres. At the age of seven, he was sent by his mother to study at an orphanage in Tirana. Later in childhood, together with his two brothers, he was engaged in heavy physical labour. After the occupation of Albania by the Italians, he participated in the partisan movement as part of the 22nd Brigade. He demonstrated heroism and fearlessness, and was appointed commissar of the

Nëndetsja 105 me Nr Luftarak 325 "RRUFEJA" prodhuar në vitin 1955 në kantierin Gorki (mbi Vollgë) në ish Bashkimin Sovjetik.

- Rreshtuar në Forcat Ushtarako Detare Shqiptare – Brigada e Nëndetsëve më 21 Shtator 1958.
- Nxjerrë nga përdorimi luftarak më 1998.
- Nëndetse e mesme detare e projektit C 613 (S613) klasi WISKI.

Gjatësia		76. m
Gjerësia		6.3m
Lartësia		14.7m
Peshkimi		5. m
Tonazhi mbi ujë		1045 t
Tonazhi nën ujë		1347 t
Thellësia maksimale e zhytjes		200 m
Shpejtësia maksimale mbi ujë		18 nyje
Shpejtesia maksimale nën ujë		13 nyje
Ekuipazhi	- Oficerë	11
	-Nënoficerë	9
	-Detarë	38

Autonomia e lundrimit 30 ditë

Bateritë
Bateri acide 2 grupe x 110 copë = 220 copë
Tension 2.5 volt Fuqia 6000 Amper

The photograph of the museum submarine with the 'movie' pennant number 105 is accompanied by a description of the submarine *Rrufeja*, which allegedly became a museum exhibit. (Photo via www.balancer.ru)

Djemal Shani – the first commander of the Submarine Brigade of the Albanian Navy (via "Detaria Shqiptare ne Rrjedhen e Kohes", 2018)

partisan detachment. After the liberation of Albania from the occupiers, he was awarded several orders and medals. As part of a group of 10 young Albanian partisans who had proven themselves during the fighting, he was sent for training in Baku to the Caspian Higher Naval Red Banner School, named after S. M. Kirov.[14] It was there that the core leaders of the Albanian Navy was formed. Djemal Shani studied in Baku for five years. It is interesting to note that his friend, the future commander of the Albanian Naval Combat Fleet, Admiral Abdi Mati, trained together with Shani. After studying in Baku, Shani continued his education at the Naval Academy named after K. E. Voroshilov of the Order of Lenin, in Leningrad. In the autumn of 1957, after the decision to appoint him the commander of the Submarine Brigade, he oversaw the selection of cadets for six-month training in the Sevastopol 11th submarine training squad. After a stay in Sevastopol, together with future Albanian submariners, Shani went to Kaliningrad, where he took part in the already described historical transition for the Albanian fleet of 4 Project 613 submarines to Pasha Liman.

In addition to commanding the Submarine Brigade, he also subsequently commanded the naval base at Pasha Liman. Djemal Shani's career in the Navy was relatively short-lived, for as a result of behind-the-scenes games and intrigues, he was forced to resign while being a Captain 1st Class, and was sent to civil service in Durres as the head of a fishing industry (He was lucky and 'only' became a 'civilian': in Albania under Hoxha of the 1950-1980s, many military personnel suffered from repressions along the Soviet patterns from the 1930s-1940s). In his new service, Shani showed his best side, modernising the fishing fleet and significantly improving the living and working conditions of fishermen. As one of the fisheries engineers later recalled: 'Djemal Shani pulled us out of slavery and restored self-esteem to ordinary fishermen'. The 'old cadres' of the fishing industry did not like this and a case was fabricated against Djemal Shani; as a result of the trial, he was fired at a fairly young age. Despite the fact that Djemal Shani repeatedly became a victim of unfair accusations and intrigues, he invariably enjoyed the respect of his former colleagues and subordinates. He died in 1993. Shani remains unforgotten by the Albanian Navy. During a commemorative ceremony in September 2022, he was posthumously awarded a 'Certificate of Honor' ('*Certifikata të Mirënjohjes*').

Service history of Albanian Whiskeys

Stuhia

Submarine *S-241* was laid down on 30 August 1955, at shipyard No.444, named after A. Marty in the city of Nikolaev. It was launched on 23 January 1956 and commissioned into service on 29 May 1956. Temporarily included in the Soviet Black Sea Fleet on 9 June 1956, in the autumn of 1956 she moved (using internal water communications of the USSR) to the Baltic Sea, and joined the Red Banner Soviet Baltic Fleet on 12 November 1956. In August 1958, the submarine transferred to the Pasha Liman base in Albania, where a joint Soviet-Albanian crew was formed to train Albanian sailors. In 1959-1960 she took part in joint manoeuvres with the Soviet Black Sea Fleet and carried out training torpedo firing. She became a part of the Albanian fleet in May 1961 under the name *Stuhia* (Albanian for 'Storm'). During its service, the submarine repeatedly changed her pennant number: 516, 241, 196, 250. 423, 305, 331, 124, 126, 316, 412, 600.

The best-documented episode of the submarine's service is the description of the record 22-day sortie of August 1969, which took place mainly along the coast of Italy. By that time, the submarine had been commanded by Aleko Pojani for 10 years, who described this sortie as a challenge to Soviet revisionists and American imperialists. The last time Albanian sailors went to sea for such a long underwater passage was in 1959, together with the Soviet captain V.S. Kozlov on

Stuhia with a pennant number 126 at sea. (via www.balancer.ru)

Another shot of *Stuhia* with a pennant number 126 at sea. (via www.balancer.ru)

the submarine *S-360* (*Vetëtima*). The voyage took place in difficult conditions, the temperature in the compartments ranged from 40 to 43 degrees Celsius, but the Albanian sailors completed the tasks assigned to them and gained invaluable experience.[15]

Aleko Pojani was perhaps the most famous submariner in Albania, who, while commanding *Stuhia*, experienced many interesting incidents and events. For example, in March 1964, the submarine surfaced in severely bad weather and Pojani was hit by a strong wave and thrown off the bridge. The boat commander miraculously managed to cling to one of the side rails and did not fall into the water. Pojani talks in detail about his service in the navy in his book *Submarine 105: Memoirs of a Commander*, which will be described later.

Stuhia with a pennant number 600, in 1985. (via www.balancer.ru)

As for *Stuhia*, she faithfully served in the fleet until 1995. After this, as described earlier, the boat was turned into a museum.

Unfortunately, in recent years the museum submarine has been kept afloat only thanks to the enthusiasm and help of private individuals and former sailors rather than government help. The submarine is heavily rusted and may sink if urgent measures are not taken.

Second commander of the submarine *Stuhia* and commander of the Submarine Brigade in 1974-1977, Aleko Pojani was born on 23 November 1937, in Tirana. He completed elementary education in Korça, after which he entered the Skënderbej military school, where he trained from 1949 to 1953. After that, he went to study in Baku at the Caspian Higher Naval Red Banner School, named after S. M. Kirov, which he graduated from in 1958 with honours. From 1958 to 1977 he served in the Submarine Brigade. It is believed that Aleko Pojani was the youngest submarine commander of an Albanian submarine (became commander at the age of 21). From 1977 to 1991 he headed the department at the Maritime Academy in Vlore, where in 1986 he defended his dissertation and received the degree of candidate of military sciences, subsequently receiving a doctorate. He became widely known as the author of the book *Submarine 105: Memoirs of a Commander* published in 2013. He died 11 July 2018.[16]

Tufani

Submarine *S-242* of Project 613 was laid down on 28 September 1955, at shipyard No.444, named after A. Marty, in the city of Nikolaev. It was launched on 29 March 1956, and entered service on 30 June 1956. The submarine was temporarily included in the Soviet Black Sea Fleet on 18 July 1956, in the summer and autumn of 1956 she moved to the Baltic Sea, and joined the Red Banner Soviet Baltic Fleet on 12 November 1956. In August 1958, she moved to the Pasha Liman base, where a joint Soviet-Albanian crew was formed to train Albanian sailors. In 1959-1960 she took part in joint manoeuvres with the Soviet Black Sea Fleet and carried out training torpedo firing. She became part of the Albanian fleet in May 1961 under the name *Tufani* ('Windstorm'). During her service, the submarine

Above: *Stuhia* under museum pennant number 105, in the spring of 2022. (via www.news.com.au)

Left: Inside the museum submarine *Stuhia*. (via Albanian Internet)

Second commander of *Stuhia*, and commander of the Submarine Brigade in 1974-1977, Aleko Pojani. (via www.pelasgoskoritsas.gr)

changed her pennant number several times: 510, 315, 332. According to some sources, she was withdrawn from the Albanian Navy by 1976, according to others, she underwent long-term repairs in 1988 but never sailed again. She was disposed of in 2011.

Rrufeja

Submarine *S-358* of Project 613 was laid down on 3 January 1955 at the Baltic Shipyard No.189, named after S. Ordzhonikidze, in the city of Leningrad. She was launched on 1 October 1955, commissioned on 24 May 1956, and on 6 August 1956 she became a part of the Red Banner Soviet Baltic Fleet. In August 1958, she moved to the Pasha Liman base, where a joint Soviet-Albanian crew was formed to train Albanian sailors. In 1959-1960 she took part in joint manoeuvres with the Soviet Black Sea Fleet and carried out training torpedo firing. She became a part of the Albanian fleet in May 1961 under the name *Rrufeja* ('Lightning'). During her service, the submarine changed her pennant number several times: 514, 552, 422, S33, 022, 325, 333. The submarine served in the Albanian Navy until 1995 and was disposed of in 2011.

Vetëtima

The Project 613 submarine *S-360* was laid down on 17 March 1955 at the Baltic Shipyard No.189, named after S. Ordzhonikidze, in the city of Leningrad. Launched on 29 April 1955, she was commissioned into service on 29 September 1956 and became a part of the Red Banner Baltic Fleet on 6 October 1956. In August 1958, she moved to the Pasha Liman base, where a joint Soviet-Albanian crew was formed to train Albanian sailors. In November-December 1959 *S-360* (under the command of Captain 3rd Rank V.S. Kozlov) made the first trip among the brigade's boats to the Mediterranean Sea towards Gibraltar. On the way back, in the Strait of Tunis, the submarine found herself next to the American cruiser USS *Des*

Albanian submarine *Rrufeja*. (via Albanian Internet)

Four *Whiskey* submarines of the Albanian Navy. (Photo via Albanian Internet)

Moines, on board of which was US President Eisenhower. She was pursued by American anti-submarine ships for three days. She became a part of the Albanian fleet in May 1961 under the name *Vetëtima* ('Lightning Strike'). During her service, the submarine repeatedly changed her pennant number: 512, 523, 442, 024, 105, 107, 335, 334. In the summer of 1967, a tragic incident occurred with the submarine while she was staying at the naval base in Pasha Liman. During the charging of its batteries, due to insufficient ventilation of the environment inside the submarine, an explosion occurred. As a result, three sailors died and two were injured. The boat was restored after major repairs by Chinese specialists. The boat served in the Albanian Navy until 1995 and was disposed of in 2011.

Summing up the story about the service of *Whiskey* submarines in the Albanian Navy, we note that these submarines theoretically could carry out combat missions throughout the Mediterranean, but in practice this was impossible due to the lack of external and combat support outside their waters. In the context of rapidly progressing NATO anti-submarine defence, Albanian submarines became more of a symbol of the Albanian naval force, rather than a real combat value asset. At the turn of the 1970-1980s, Hoxha claimed that the Albanian fleet controlled the Strait of Otranto, but this did not correspond to reality. NATO ships and, above all, the Italian Navy, had detection and destruction means that ensured the elimination of surface and underwater targets at a distance many times greater than the torpedo attack range of the Albanian submarines and torpedo boats. Italian Air Force fighter-bombers and Navy helicopters were also trained to fight the boats of the Albanian fleet that lacked anti-ship missiles.

However, the actual main purpose of the Albanian four submarines was primarily to fulfil a propaganda goal, the need to show 'American imperialists and Soviet revisionists' (and after 1978 also to Chinese 'traitors') the ability of a tiny country to maintain a submarine fleet and send it for 'demonstrations of power' into neighbouring seas. It is not for nothing that an Albanian *Whiskey* submarine became the 'main character' of the monumental film *Face to Face*.

Concluding this chapter on Albanian submarines, one cannot help but note the remarkable efforts of Chinese specialists and industry during the reign of Comrade Mao that helped to build the necessary infrastructure to support the operation of the Albanian submarines, to train the relevant personnel and to localise the production of the spare parts.

2

BULGARIAN *GLORY* AND *VICTORY*

It may seem surprising, but the commencement of the submarine service in the Bulgarian Navy dates back to the very beginning of the 20th Century. The first naval submarine officer was Lieutenant Rashko Serafimov, who was trained in the French Navy and practised on the Russian submarines. During the First World War, in which Bulgaria participated on the side of the Central Powers, the German submarine UB I-8 was purchased for the Bulgarian fleet. With the commissioning of Submarine No.18 into the navy on 25 May 1916, Bulgaria became one of the few European countries to have submarines. After the defeat in the First World War, as well as following the results of the Second World War, Bulgaria was prohibited from having submarines in service. Only the changing political conditions of the mid-1950s allowed the Bulgarian submarine fleet to be built again, with submarines supplied by the Soviet Union.

Despite the fact that the first submarines officially became a part of the Bulgarian Navy only in 1954, the training of Bulgarian submariners began, in fact, six years earlier. In the spring of 1948, after secret negotiations between the USSR and the People's Republic of Bulgaria, the latter started recruiting sailors for training on the Soviet torpedo boats and submarines. By 15 April 1948, after a two-day passage on the motor ship *Belorussia*, groups of Bulgarian cadets arrived at the Odessa naval base of the Soviet Black Sea Fleet. It was there that the training of Bulgarian submariners began for the first time after a 30-year break. At the beginning of June of the same year, the training of Bulgarian sailors began in Arbuznaya Gavan on submarines of M-class submarines (XV series), also known as *Malyutka*-class, from the Second Odessa Separate Division with pennant numbers: *M-202*, *M-203* and *M- 204*. By 1951, the crews of the submarines were completely Bulgarian, but for political reasons the submarines were included in the Soviet Navy. It was then that the officer core of the submarine forces of the Bulgarian fleet was formed, since most of the future commanders of the Bulgarian submarines were trained or served on *Malyutkas* as a part of the Soviet fleet.[1]

Finally, by 1954, all formalities for having submarines as a part of the Bulgarian Navy were settled, and on 18 August 1954, at the Varna base, the naval flags of Bulgaria were solemnly raised on three submarines of *Malyutka* type and documents were signed on their gratuitous transfer and acceptance into the Bulgarian Navy. By order of the Minister of Defence on this day, the 8th Separate Submarine Division was created, the commander of which was directly subordinate to the commander of the Bulgarian fleet.

Obviously, *Malyutkas* built during the Second World War could no longer pose a serious threat to a potential enemy, so in 1958 Bulgaria received from the Soviet Black Sea Fleet two modern submarines *S-244* and *S-245* (both commissioned in 1956) of Project 613, which received in the Bulgarian Navy pennant numbers *S-41* and *S-42* and the names *Slava* and *Pobeda*, respectively. The submarines *M-202* and *M-203* were decommissioned and transferred to the Soviet Black Sea Fleet for scrapping, while *M-204* was converted into a floating charging station.

The first commander of the submarine *S-41* was Captain-Lieutenant Todor Georgiev, and the first commander of the submarine *S-42* was Captain-Lieutenant Ivan Fidanchev (future rear admiral).

Two Bulgarian Malyutkas in the port of Varna. (via www.morskivestnik.com)

The solemn ceremony of acceptance of *Whiskey* submarines into the Bulgarian Navy on 12 September 1958. Naval flags are carried by two commanders of the boats, namely, Captain-Lieutenant Ivan Fidanchev and Captain-Lieutenant Todor Georgiev. (via www.morskivestnik.com)

The new submarines of the Bulgarian fleet on 12 September 1958. (via www.morskivestnik.com)

The submarines were officially commissioned into the Bulgarian Navy on 20 September 1958, along with several other warships received from the USSR, including one Project 50 patrol ship (ASCC/NATO reporting name: *Riga*-class).

The new vessels were a huge breakthrough for the Bulgarian fleet, but at the same time they caused a number of issues, primarily due to the large number of technological innovations and the need to triple the number of officers on board (compared to *Malyutkas*). A shortage of officers meant that they had to be transferred to submarines from surface ships. However, despite the difficulties, the Bulgarians quickly mastered the submarines and by December 1958, active campaigns and exercises at sea began. These successfully continued throughout the 1960s, when the submarines were already in full combat readiness.

The command of the Bulgarian Navy attached particular importance to the readiness of the *Whiskey* submarines, which were combat-ready on average 90-120 days per year. The submarines took mandatory part in the annual manoeuvres of the Bulgarian fleet. The command of the Bulgarian fleet regularly sent submarines to the Turkish shores towards the Bosporus on 5–10 days expeditions, primarily for reconnaissance purposes. Subsequently, the submarines trained in combat missions in various remote (from Bulgaria) parts of the Black Sea. The training included staying under water for 15-20 days.[2]

As the anti-submarine forces of the Bulgarian Navy strengthened, submarines were involved in joint exercises with submarine hunters (including ASW helicopters). In particular, those were the exercises Rodopi in 1967, Pliska in 1968, and Preslav in 1971. Over the course of 13 years of active service in the Bulgarian Navy, Project 613 submarines successfully demonstrated themselves in various exercises and manoeuvres. It is worth noting that both vessels underwent annual inspections and minor repairs in Sevastopol, and the first serious intermediate repairs of the submarines were carried out in the period 1966-1968 in Varna, at the Flotsky Arsenal shipyard. The submarines were withdrawn from the Bulgarian fleet in the summer of 1972, when they were replaced by two Soviet-made Project 633 (NATO reporting name: *Romeo*-class) submarines.

Service history of Bulgarian Whiskeys

Slava

The submarine *S-244* was laid down on 14 December 1955 in Nikolaev. It was launched on 12 April 1956, entered service on 31 August 1956 and was included in the Soviet Black Sea Fleet. On 12 September 1958, the submarine was transferred to the Bulgarian Navy and received the name *Slava* ('Glory') and pennant number 41.

The submarine was withdrawn from service on 28 May 1972, returned to the USSR and was stripped for metal in 1973.

During its service in the Bulgarian Navy, *Slava* was commanded by the following officers:

1958-1961 – Captain-Lieutenant Todor Hristov Georgiev
1961-1962 – Captain 3rd rank Gutsan Stoikov Gutsanov

Submarine *Slava* in 1972. (via www.blackseavisits.ru)

An interesting photograph from 1962: on board submarine *Slava*. Her first commander Todor Georgiev is in the centre, who by that time had become the chief of staff of the Submarine Division, and his successor, Gutsan Gutsanov, is on the right. (via www.morskivestnik.com)

1962-1968 – Captain 3rd rank Vasil Nikolov Lazarov
1968-1971 – Captain 3rd rank Konstantin Evstatiev Ploshchakov
1971-1972 – Captain 3rd rank Anton Vasilev Yankulov

Konstantin Evstatyev Ploshakov was born on 17 January 1934 in the town of Strelcha, Plovdiv region. He graduated from the Higher Naval School from 1949 to 1953. Subsequently, he graduated from the officer courses for submarine commanders in 1963 and the Naval Academy in Leningrad in 1965-1968. He was a commander of the Bulgarian Navy submarine *S-41 Slava* from 1968 to 1971. He gained publicity as a writer and marine painter, and was a member of the Union of Bulgarian Writers and was an author of seven novels and one short story, three collections of short stories and two non-fiction books. He died in 2006. According to his will, after his death his ashes were scattered in Varna Bay from submarine *Slava*, the submarine of the same name he commanded, but this time it was a Soviet Project 633 (NATO reporting name: *Romeo*-class) boat.

Konstantin Evstatyev Ploshakov – commander of the submarine *S-41 Slava* from 1968 to 1971. (via www.submariners-bg.com)

Pobeda

Submarine *S-245* was laid down on 24 December 1955 in Nikolaev, and launched on 20 April 1956, entered service on 14 September 1956 and was included in the Soviet Black Sea Fleet. On 12 September 1958, she was transferred to the Bulgarian Navy, receiving name *Pobeda* ('Victory'), pennant number 42.

On 5 December 1972, the submarine was withdrawn from the Bulgarian Navy and scrapped.

During her service in the Bulgarian Navy, *Pobeda* was commanded by the following officers:

1958-1960 – Captain-Lieutenant Ivan Dimov Fidanchev
1960-1962 – Captain 3rd Rank Rumen Georgiev Popov
1962-1964 – Captain 3rd Rank Gutsan Stoikov Gutsanov
1964-1967 – Captain 3rd Rank Kostadin Ruskov
1967-1972 – Captain 3rd Rank Ilya Ivanov Duchkov

Submarine *S-245* during testing in 1956. (Photo via the collection of V.P. Zablotsky)

Sailors of the first crew (1958-1961) of submarine *Pobeda*. (Photo via www.morskivestnik.com)

Pobeda in Varna, August 1967. (via archive of A. Andreev)

Bulgarian submarine *S-42 Pobeda*. (via www.submariners-bg.com)

Loading of a torpedo onto *Pobeda* in the open sea from the STB-606 self-propelled torpedo barge. (via www.morskivestnik.com)

The first commander of submarine *Pobeda*, Ivan Dimitrov Fidanchev. (www.submariners-bg.com)

The first commander of the Bulgarian Navy submarine *Pobeda*, Ivan Dimitrov Fidanchev, was born on 24 May 1927, in the village of Patriarshego Evtimiya, Asenovgrad region. He participated in the resistance to the government until 1944 as a partisan. He graduated from the Naval Academy, studying between 1945 to 1949. From September 1953, Senior Lieutenant Fidanchev served in the submarine division in Odessa as assistant commander of *Malyutka M-204*. From 1954 to 1958 he was a commander of *Malyutka M-43* (formerly *M-204*). From 1958 to 1960 he was a commander of *Whiskey*-class *Pobeda* submarine. From 1960 to 1963 he studied in the Naval Academy in Leningrad. From 1963 to 1967 he was a commander of the Eighth Separate Submarine Division. He completed his service in the Navy with the rank of Rear Admiral, Deputy Commander-in-Chief of the Navy in 1979. He died on 14 December 1995.

Despite the fact that the Bulgarian *Whiskey*-class submarines have received much less publicity compared to the *Romeo*-class submarines that succeeded them, it is impossible to overestimate their role in the development of the Bulgarian submarine fleet. For the first time in history, Bulgaria received submarines that could operate throughout the Black Sea and pose a threat to any warship of the Turkish Navy. We must also not forget the role of the Bulgarian *Whiskeys* as a 'training ground' for the personnel of *Romeo*-class submarines that joined Bulgarian Navy in 1970s.

Bulgarian *Whiskey*-class submarines in the port of Varna. (collection of Yu.N. Vasilchenko)

3

WHISKEY SUBMARINES IN THE LAND OF PHARAOHS

The history of Soviet military and economic cooperation with Egypt is well and thoroughly described in Russian and Western literature. It was started in the mid-1950s by N.S. Khrushchev and G.A. Nasser, and ended under President A. Sadat in the mid-1970s. The friendly relations between two countries are known primarily for the construction of the Aswan Dam and the massive use of Soviet weapons by the Egyptians in the wars with Israel. Paradoxically, the USSR often supplied Egypt with even more modern weapons than North Vietnam, but the mass of the same was of a purely defensive nature.

Information about the supply of Soviet submarines to Egypt, in principle, was not a big secret for military specialists, historians and relevant specialised publications. However, the main burden in wars with Israel has always been borne by the ground army, air force and air defence of Egypt: the role of the Egyptian Navy in the Middle East wars has always been, at most, secondary. Even the historical success of the sinking of the Israeli destroyer *Eilat* in 1967, by Soviet P-15 Termit (ASCC/NATO reporting name: *SS-N-2 Styx*) anti-ship missiles (ASMs) from the Egyptian missile boats, was more of an important page in the development and evolution of missile technology rather than a turning point in Arab-Israeli wars. This first-ever destruction of a warship by anti-ship missiles created incredible demand for the 'weapon of the poor' – missile boats that allowed cash-strapped countries to receive (presumable) protection from the fleets of major maritime powers. For decades, this 'niche' on the international market was dominated by the USSR.

Contrary to at least some operations of Soviet-made destroyers operated by the Egyptian Navy, submarine operations of the same service are next to unknown. The first negotiations on the supply of Soviet naval equipment took place in autumn 1955, when a group of high-ranking Egyptian Navy officers visited Tallinn. As a result of the visit and familiarisation with Soviet ships, the Egyptians purchased a large batch of Soviet weapons: destroyers, minesweepers, torpedo boats and, for the first time in Egyptian history, a total of three submarines. Two of them were modern Project 613 submarines and one small *Malyutka*. In attempt to lessen western sensitivities about deliveries of 'Soviet arms', the training of about 300 Egyptian officers and other ranks for destroyers and submarines took place mostly in Gdynia, Poland and only a small group of 30 Egyptian naval officers and sailors arrived to the Soviet Black Sea Fleet for training on submarines.[1] Moreover, the transfer of ships to the Egyptian Navy took place formally on the part of Poland. This was similar to the Egyptian acquisition of MiG fighter jets and tanks being masqueraded as the 'Czechoslovak Arms Deal'.[2]

Unfortunately for the Egyptians, the mass of the Soviet naval equipment came too late to take part in the Suez War of 1956. Only two Project 30-bis destroyers and several Project 183 (ASCC/NATO reporting name: *Bolshevik*-class) torpedo boats took part in the conflict and two of the latter were lost. The training of Egyptian submariners was delayed, and the vessels simply did not have time to reach Egyptian ports to engage in the conflict. According to Polish sources, the first submarine departed from Gdynia for Egypt in late October 1956, wearing the pennant number *M-107*, but due to the outbreak of war, while already in the Gibraltar area, she turned around and headed back to Poland. The submarine was accompanied by ship *BAŁTYK* under the Polish flag and had three commanders on board: Soviet (Isakov?), Polish (Leon Ratajczak) and Egyptian (Fathi Sharaki). Curiously, US sources registered this as 'attempt to reach Egypt': a week after the war was over, on 13 November, the CIA assessed that, 'the first Soviet submarine for Egypt was en route from Poland when Israel launched its offensive in the Sinai.'

History does not tolerate the subjunctive mood, but it would be interesting to see the combat operations of the newest Soviet submarines of that time against the fleets of Great Britain and France, which had colossal anti-submarine expertise. In any case, the Egyptian crews neither in 1956 nor in 1957 were ready to fully operate submarines and long after their transfer they were still honing their skills.

It was only on 6 June 1957 that the first three submarines – two Project 613, pennant numbers *S-175* and *S-182*, and one Project 96 *Malyutka* (*M-271*) left the Gulf of Gdansk, accompanied by the base minesweeper *BT-484*, and began the transition to Egypt. The crew of *M-271* was entirely Egyptian with a few Soviet officers. The large submarines each had two crews, the Soviet one controlled the boat, and the Egyptian one was in the wings, learning from the experienced crew. The transition was carried out on the surface only. On 9 June, the detachment entered the Western Mediterranean through the Strait of Gibraltar, and on 16 June, it reached Alexandria. On 21 June 1957, *S-175* and *S-182* were excluded from the Soviet Navy and officially leased by the Egyptian Navy. They were re-designated as follows:

- *S-175* = *S-1*, and
- *S-182* = *S-2*.

At the same time, the transferred *Malyutka M-271* was also stricken from the Soviet Navy and joined Egyptian fleet. The basic minesweeper *BT-484*, which escorted submarines during their passage to Alexandria, at first went to Sevastopol and then returned to Baltiysk. Officially, *S-1* and *S-2* were commissioned into service with the Egyptian Navy on 26 June 1957.

Following the results of the 1956 war, Egypt planned to further strengthen its fleet and on 3 March 1957, an agreement was signed with the USSR for the supply of three additional Project 613 submarines and 12 torpedo boats. Submarine crew training was still to take place in Gdynia, Poland.

On 3 April 1958, the Egyptian newspapers *al-Gamhuria* and *al-Chaab* reported the arrival of three *Whiskey*-class submarines in Alexandria, a day earlier. Accordingly, the boats left the Polish port of Gdansk in March 1958, the crews of the boats having been trained there. These were three Project 613 submarines from the Soviet Baltic Fleet: *S-180*, *S-193* and *S-184*. The first two were stricken from the Soviet Navy on 22 April 1958, leased to the Egyptian Navy and assigned the numbers *S-3* and *S-4*. The third was stricken from the Soviet Navy on 24 April 1958, was leased to the Egyptian Navy and renamed as *S-5*.

Even after the transfer of the submarines to the Egyptian Navy, Soviet sailors continued to assist the Egyptian crews in mastering the boats, because, often, the qualifications of the Egyptian sailors were not up to par. There are memoirs of the retired submariner Captain 2nd Rank M.I. Saranchuk about his 'business trip' to Egypt in 1959, where he shared his experience with local sailors. By that time, Captain 2nd Rank Saranchuk had seven years of experience in commanding submarines of *Shchuka*- and *Whiskey*-classes. Among other incidents, he recalled:

Former Soviet Project 96 submarine *Malyutka M-271* as a part of the Egyptian Navy in 1957. 'Simpler' if compared to *Whiskey* submarines, she was the first submarine mastered by an Egyptian crew and became the first combat-ready submarine of the Egyptian Navy. In the 1960s she was used as a training submarine. (via www.deepstorm.ru)

One of the first two *Whiskey* submarines of the Egyptian Navy during the filming of the 1957 comedy movie *Ismail Yassin in the Navy*. (via www.forums.airbase.ru)

> As a combat training adviser, I strove to ensure that the Arabs not only mastered diving the boat, but also learned to use submarine weapons. On one of the submarines, I went to sea so that I could be at sea for as long as possible, and especially in a submerged position. There was an experienced submarine mechanic Ivan Mikhailovich Plotnikov in the submarine with me and a military translator from Arabic – a young man who was on the ship for the first time. The rest were the regular Arab crew – 52 people. From the first steps, the poor organisation of the service and the uncertain actions of the crew and officers, including the submarine commander, were noticeable. There was a lack of practical skills when executing commands so all manoeuvres were carried out carefully without haste... The voyage was simple and without incidents. But staying under water for three days was very difficult for the crew, which did not have any practical skills in this. Suffice it to remember that during this short period there were ten cases of fainting in the submarine, nine times the commander asked permission to surface. The main reasons: inappropriate food – low in calories and monotonous, poor physical condition of most crew members, low level of sanitation and personal hygiene. Constant depression and drowsiness of most crew members, with an increased content of carbon dioxide in the compartments. Muslims in the submarine compartments did not know which way to face when performing *namaz*; they did not have the opportunity to perform a full ritual in difficult and unusual conditions for them, when they needed the help of Allah. Overcoming difficulties, the crew carried out the plan – they were underwater for three days, newspapers published about this even before the submarine returned to Alexandria. This was a previously unattainable result, the first success...Acting as an adviser, by the end of 1959 we managed to carry out torpedo firing on four submarines in simple conditions.[3]

The memoirs of M.I. Saranchuk are interesting with the following description:

> [O]n each arriving submarine, several Soviet officers and midshipmen were left to train Arab specialists in servicing instruments and mechanisms. Over the course of two months, the organisation of the duty and watch service when the submarine was moored at the pier was also worked out. This was the end of the mission of Soviet specialists; then the Egyptians were left to continue on their own. To eliminate various breakdowns and malfunctions of complex mechanisms, there was a team of specialists who arrived from the factories where the submarines were built.

The next stage of deliveries of submarines to the Egyptian Navy occurred in 1962, when the supply of submarines was carried out along with the transfer of two Project 30-bis destroyers to Egypt. The situation with the transfer of submarines is not entirely clear as it remains unknown whether one or two boats were supplied. In the memoirs of Admiral V. Kozlov, *Underwater War: Horizons of the great Confrontation between the Superpowers*, who was then senior officer at the mentioned transfer, the delivery of two *Whiskey* submarines to Egypt is confirmed. The study by George S. Dragnich, 'The Soviet Union's quest for access to naval facilities in Egypt prior to the June war of 1967' also mentions the transfer of two "W" class submarines to Alexandria in January 1962 and two *Skory*-class destroyers in January 1962. However, western publications reported only the arrival of one submarine in Alexandria, and it is known that only *S-228* from the Red Banner Baltic Fleet was stricken from the Soviet Navy on 19 January 1962 and sold to Egypt, where she received the designation *S-6*.

On 17 July 1965 Egyptian troop transport *El Quseir* accompanied by two Egyptian *Whiskey*-class submarines (*S-3* and *S-4*) entered the Baltic Sea and headed for the Soviet ports for repairs. At the same time, the Egyptians were about to receive two additional *Whiskey* boats: *S-226* and *S-227* were transferred from the Soviet Baltic Fleet, following overhauls at the Shipyard No.177, in Ust-Dvinsk (nowadays Daugavgrīva, Latvia). An amount of 350,000 rubles was allocated for the repair of each submarine.[4]

According to the memoirs of retired Captain 1st Rank A.A. Bederov, who was then the head of the technical department of the Riga Logistics Department of the Soviet Baltic Fleet:

> The very first submarines went to Egypt under their own power with our (Soviet) crews. Those two, which were drawn up with my assistance (he means here *S-226* and *S-227*), the Egyptians decided to overtake right in Riga…For this purpose, a mother ship and two worn-out boats of Project 613, which we handed over to them three years ago, came to us. One should take a lot of effort to bring these boats to the point of complete wear and tear! I was ordered to restore the bilge pump that failed during the transition and install navigation equipment on the Egyptian mother ship, for which I arrived on the ship.[5]

For the sake of objectivity, one should keep in mind that by 1965 the boats *S-3* and *S-4* had served already in the Egyptian Navy not for three, but for 7 years.

The abovementioned *S-226* and *S-227* were taken by the Egyptian crews and arrived in Alexandria on 25 December 1965, where they became *S-7* and *S-8*, respectively. On 29 April 1966, the Egyptian submarines *S-3* (*S-180* leased in 1958) and *S-4* (*S-193* leased in 1958) were returned to the Soviet Union and re-enlisted in the Soviet Baltic Fleet: the former became *UTS-36* and the latter *UTS-37* – where UTS stood for *Учебно-Тренировочное Судно*, meaning 'Training Vessel'.

On 24 August 1966, the Egyptian submarine *S-1* (former Soviet *S-175*, leased in 1957) was returned to the USSR and re-enlisted in the Soviet Baltic Fleet under the designation *S-42*. She became the third Egyptian submarine previously leased and returned by the Egyptians to the USSR during 1966. Project 613 submarines were, by agreement, replaced by more modern Project 633 (NATO reporting name: *Romeo*-class) boats.

The Egyptian submarine fleet before the start of the June 1967 Arab-Israeli War consisted of 11 boats. Five of them from the Project 613 (*S-2, S-5, S-6, S-7, S-8*), five from the Project 633 (*Romeo*-class) and a training *Malyutka* of Project 96. This is according to Soviet statistical data regarding supplies to Egypt, and is considered true and accurate. There are, however, some reliable sources that indicate the Egyptian Navy also comprised at least two more Whiskeys confiscated from the Syrian Navy (Below, in the chapter related to the Syrian submarines, this will be further described). According to the article "Naval Aspects of the 1967 War" by the Egyptian Admiral Ashraf M. Refaat, two Egyptian submarines were based in the Red Sea.[6] The author assumes that these were *Whiskey* submarines, since all five *Romeo*-class vessels had been in the Egyptian Navy for less than a year at the beginning of the war, most likely less mastered at that time and, finally, as more modern, should have been used in the more important Mediterranean theatre. All that remains is to understand which *Whiskeys* were on the Red Sea. Considering that soon after the war *S-2* and S-5 returned to the Baltic (it is unlikely that they would have made such a route around Africa due to the blocked Suez Canal), only three others were left: *S-6*, *S-7*, and *S-8*. Based on currently available information, no additional conclusions are possible. Of course, we also should keep in mind two more ex-Syrian Whiskeys.

The only offensive operation of the Egyptian underwater fleet was the dispatch of three submarines to the Israeli shores on 6 June 1967: one north of Haifa, another south of Haifa, and a third near Ashdod. They made not a single attack, since the Israelis stopped all

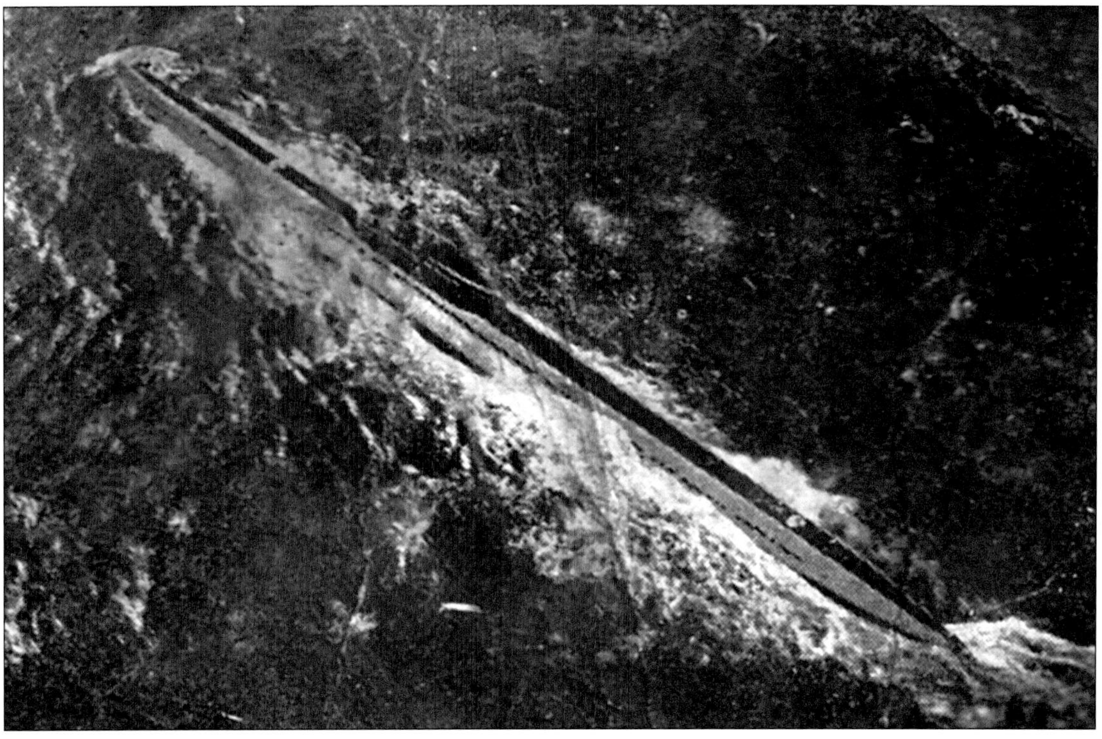

An image of one of the Egyptian *Whiskey* submarines on the Egyptian Army field propaganda postcard as of 1967. (Nour Bardai collection)

international traffic. Moreover, the tactics of Egyptian submariners was at the level of the Second World War; they very often unnecessarily used periscopes for orientation, not trusting modern equipment, which ultimately led to the detection of the boats.

On the morning of 6 June, an Israeli patrol vessel near Haifa discovered a periscope sticking out of the water and sounded alarm. Destroyers *Eilat*, *Jaffa* and the patrol ship *Nogah* went on the search. Surface ships discovered and attacked an Egyptian submarine off Ashdod. According to the Israelis, some oil products came to the surface after the attack, and they believed that they damaged the submarine. A second engagement took place around noon of 7 June. The Israeli frigate *Haifa*, which was on patrol in the Haifa area, spotted two Egyptian submarines near the Lebanese border and immediately attacked them with depth charges. One of the submarines left at high speed, and the second, according to Israeli data, was damaged and was forced to return to base. As a result of the attack, an oil slick was observed on the surface of the sea. According to Israeli data, it was a Project 633 submarine with pennant number 24. The Egyptian Navy, however, has never confirmed damage or loss of any of its submarines.[7]

Another contemporary source concluded:

> The only offensive operation of the Egyptian fleet that attracted the attention of the Israelis was undertaken on June 6, when three submarines approached the Israeli shores: one appeared north of Haifa, another south of Haifa, and a third near Ashdod. It is unclear whether the Egyptians intended to attack Israeli ships or land saboteurs, as the Israelis did at Port Said and Alexandria. The Israeli Navy had only four sonars, but the Israeli sailors managed to detect all three Egyptian submarines and attack them with depth charges. There is no doubt that one of them, judging by the large oil slick that floated to the surface, was damaged. However, all three boats managed to escape. General Harel, commander of the Israeli navy, commented afterwards: 'They overused their periscopes. With the technology that the Egyptians had, they could have picnics on the outskirts of Haifa'.[8]

With a high degree of probability, some of the boats sent to the shores of Israel were *Whiskeys* due to their better mastery by Egyptian crews. And, of course, if skirmishes with the Israeli surface ships took place, it is surprising why modern (at that time) submarines did not attack ships built during the Second World War. Ironically, the Israeli counterattacks were carried out with depth charges, also in Second World War-style: therefore, the lack of attempts by Egyptians to attack the enemy can be explained either by the very low morale or by the lack of necessary skills.

The passivity of the Egyptian fleet and the easy victory in the war played a cruel joke on the Israeli Navy. On 21 October 1967, the Israeli destroyer *Eilat* was sunk near Port Said by three Termit anti-ship missiles fired by two Egyptian *Komar*-class missile boats.

On 14 August 1967, the Egyptian submarine *S-5* was returned to the USSR: on 24 August, she was re-commissioned to the Soviet Baltic Fleet as *S-15*. On 5 July 1968, the Egyptian submarine *S-2* was returned to and re-enlisted as *S-406*. This was the fifth and the last Egyptian *Whiskey* leased to Egypt by the Soviet Union in the 1950s returned to the USSR. As a replacement, the Egyptian Navy received more modern *Romeo*-class boats.

It is interesting to note that the Egyptians were still receiving new batches of *Whiskey* submarines. On 1 October 1971, two Project 613 submarines flying the Egyptian naval ensign were spotted passing the Strait of Dover. These were *S-280* and *S-380* from the Soviet Baltic Fleet; upon arrival in Alexandria, they were handed over to the Egyptians: *S-280* became *S-28* and received pennant number 415, and *S-380* became *S-29* and received pennant number 418.

As per the use of Egyptian submarines between 1967 and 1973, perhaps the most striking episode was an affair that took place on 17 April 1973. As the British liner *Queen Elizabeth 2* was underway from UK to Ashdod in Israel, carrying a big party to celebrate the 25th anniversary of the founding of the State of Israel, the Libyan leader Muamar el-Qadhafi summoned the commander of the Egyptian Navy's submarine based in his country at the time. The stunned Egyptian then received an oral order to sink the ship to avenge the tragic and mistaken downing of a Libyan passenger Boeing 727 by an Israeli jet over Sinai on 21 February 1973. He reacted by asking for a written order and, after receiving it, went to the sea. After spending almost a day under water, the submarine surfaced and sent a radiogram to Egyptian President Anwar Sadat about the planned attack. Sadat instantly cancelled the attack and ordered a return to the port of Alexandria. Sometime later, when *QE 2* left potentially dangerous waters, Sadat informed Qadhafi that the submarine was unable to detect the liner.[9]

Next to nothing is known about the participation of the Egyptian submarines in the October 1973 Arab-Israeli War. The minimal available information is unstructured and often contradictory. According to the former Israeli President, retired Major General and historian Chaim Herzog:

> At the beginning of the war, the Egyptians deployed their submarines east of Crete, but most of the time they scoured the seas without any result, with the exception of the sinking of two innocent Greek cargo ships – one in the northwest of Alexandria, the other even further west. As Israeli troops advanced and the threat to the Egyptian coast increased, some of the submarines were recalled to coastal waters.[10]

On the other hand, the commander of the Egyptian fleet, Admiral Fuad Zukri, said in an interview that the Egyptian submarines, 'went on the attack three times during the war – on October 7, 11 and 22'.[11] Interestingly, one of the two sunken Greek cargo ships that Chaim Herzog mentioned was sunk on 25 October, and, based on the words of the Egyptian admiral, it was definitely not the Egyptians who sank her. The Israelis also deny the attack of their submarines on the unlucky 'neutral', which was carrying cargo from warring Alexandria in Egypt to Benghazi in Libya.

Before the start of the war, Egypt had 11 combat-ready submarines directly supplied from the USSR (five *Whiskey*-class and six *Romeo*-class). There were also two more *Whiskey*-class boats captured from Syrians in Egyptian possession. As a result of the Six-Day War, the Suez Canal was blocked for passage of all ships. Certainly enough, this did not stop the Egyptians, and they transferred submarines to the Red Sea from the Mediterranean around Africa.[12] Accordingly, it can be assumed that the Egyptian fleet in the Red Sea received additional vessels. In fact, the famous Egyptian resource 'group73historians.com' discusses only two *Romeo*-class boats in the Red Sea. That would leave seven *Whiskey*-class and four *Romeo*-class submarines in the Mediterranean. The Egyptian source gives highly interesting information that two 'Improved *Whiskeys*' received in 1971, went on two eventually failed missions to mine the port of Haifa during the war: *S-28* on the morning 5 October, *S-29* in the evening of 7 October. Both boats had 8 mines which they eventually cleared into the sea. Furthermore, the source describes that, during the morning of 11 October, *S-29* launched two torpedoes at an unidentified ship at North Sinai and an explosion was heard.[13] The strategy of deploying submarines and capital ships of the Egyptian fleet in 1973 differed significantly from earlier times. Perhaps for the first time in the history of conflicts with Israel, the Egyptian fleet was clearly given a goal to fulfill. And, as subsequent events showed, its implementation played an important role in the conflict. This task was to block sea routes to Israeli ports in order to prevent the supply of weapons and fuel during the war. Consequently, only one or two merchants were able to reach Israel by the Red Sea, and only 17 (according to Israeli data: '80') by the Mediterranean.

The role of Egyptian submarines was less significant than that of the surface fleet. In the Mediterranean Sea, most of them operated closer to the Israeli shores than destroyers, which already guaranteed far fewer potential targets for interception. In addition, the submarine is objectively less suitable for stopping and inspecting civilian ships compared to destroyers. Most importantly, the Egyptians could not wage unrestricted submarine warfare like the Germans in the Atlantic or the Americans in the Pacific during the Second World War. President Sadat was less militant than Nasser and tried to avoid internationalising the conflict. With military targets, the situation was even worse for the Egyptian submarines: Israel decommissioned its large surface ships before the war began and it was close to impossible to hunt the tiny high-speed missile boats, especially in the coastal waters. Israel still had two submarines, constructed during the Second World War, but there were no known encounters with them. There were even fewer prospects for Egyptian submarines in the Red Sea. As can be clearly seen from the accompanying map, Egyptian submarines patrolled the central part of the Red Sea.[14] However, three Egyptian capital ships were operating further south, blocking the narrow Bab el-Mandeb Strait, intercepting 99% of the ships heading to the Red Sea.

Consequently, Egyptian submarines did not play any significant role in the 1973 conflict. The geopolitical situation and changes in Israeli naval doctrine forced Egyptian submarines to become almost useless weapons. Egyptian admirals could have taken the risk of

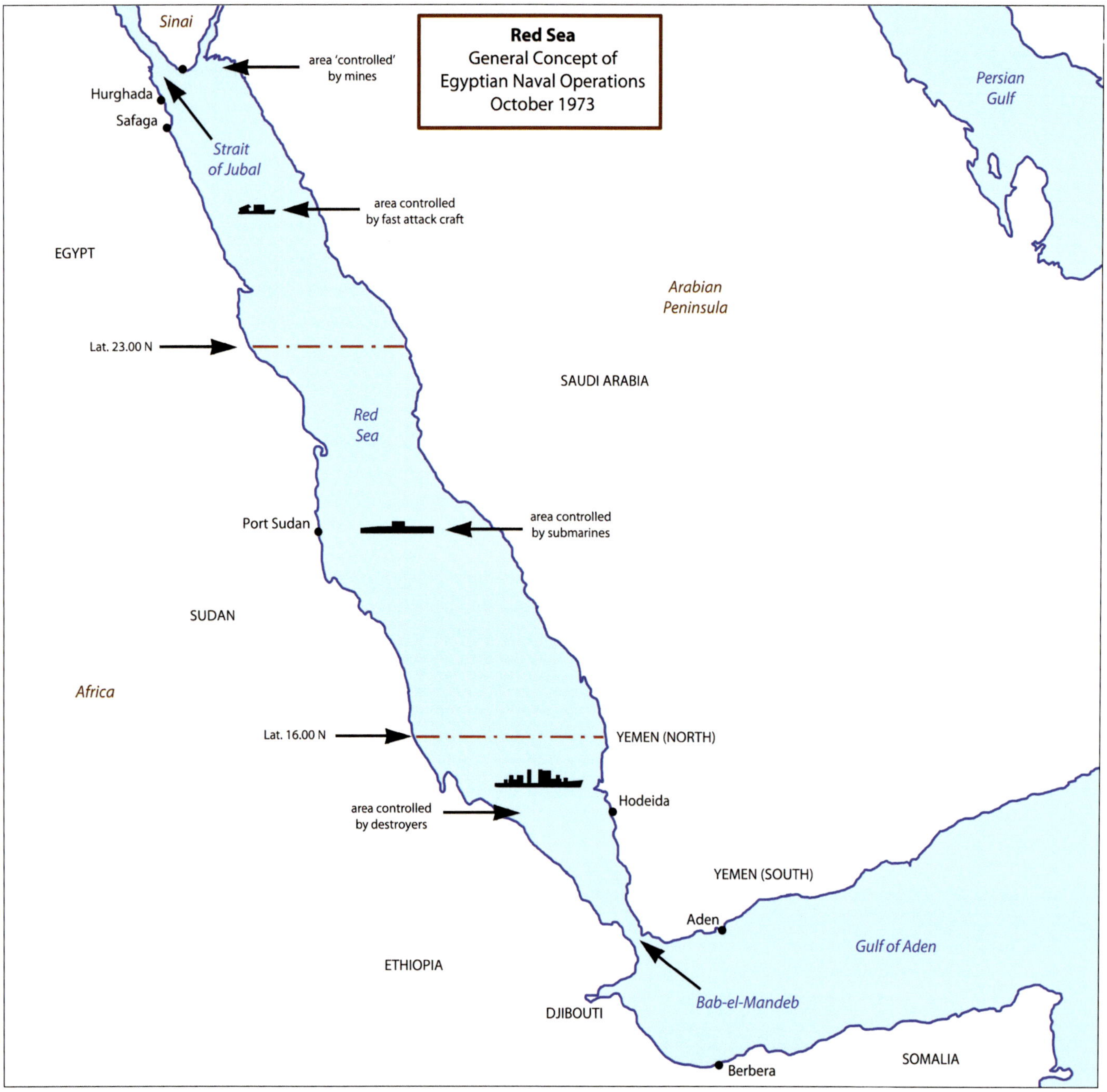

Egyptian warships in the Red Sea during the Yom Kippur War of 1973. (b.b.h.illustrations based on article of Egyptian Admiral Ashraf M. Refaat)

sending a couple of boats very close to Israel's Mediterranean ports to lay mines or attack ships near the harbours. The loss of one or two boats would not have negatively affected the Egyptian navy, but could have greatly complicated the functioning of both the military and civilian services of Israeli ports. In any case, the Egyptian fleet fully completed its task of blocking Israeli ports, and Egyptian submarines played a role, albeit a secondary one. A little-known fact is that the first demand of the Israelis during the ceasefire negotiations was the opening of the Bab el-Mandeb Strait to shipping, since Israel's fuel reserves were practically running out.

Service history of Egyptian Whiskeys

S-1

Submarine *S-175* of project 613 was laid down on 31 October 1953 at the shipbuilding plant No.112 Krasnoye Sormovo, named after A.A. Zhdanov, in the city of Gorky. She was launched on 16 March 1954. In the spring of 1954, she was moved to Leningrad to undergo acceptance tests. She was commissioned on 16 October 1954, and on 19 October 1954 she became a part of the IV Fleet (from 24 December 1955 the Red Banner Baltic Fleet). On 26 June 1957, she entered service with the Egyptian Navy on lease. After nine years of service in Egypt, she was returned to the Soviet Union and again became a part of the Soviet Baltic Fleet as *S-42*. On 25 May 1970, she was withdrawn from the list of submarines and converted into a floating charging station *PZS-41* based in Liepaja. In 1977, she was reorganised into a raid floating charging station, *RPZS-411*. In the spring of 1979, she arrived in Cuba and became a part of the Cuban Navy as a floating charging station. She was decommissioned in the early 1990s.

S-2

Submarine *S-182* of Project 613 was laid down on 30 January 1954 at the shipbuilding plant No.112, and launched on 29 May 1954. In the summer of 1954, she was transferred down the Volga and Caspian Sea to the plant's acceptance base in the city of Baku to undergo testing. The ship entered service on 8 December 1954. On 18 December 1954, she was temporarily included in the Caspian Military Flotilla. In the summer of 1955, she was transferred via inland water systems from Baku to the city of Leningrad. Commissioned on 20 September 1955, she was assigned to the VI Fleet. On 26 June 1957, she entered service with the Egyptian Navy as *S-2*. After 11 years of service, she was returned to the Soviet Union and again joined the Soviet Baltic Fleet on 5 July 1968 as *S-406*, based in Ust-Dvinsk. Subsequently, she underwent repairs at shipyard No.177 in Ust-Dvinsk, and at the beginning of 1972 she was relocated to Liepaja. From October 1979 to February 1981, she underwent medium repairs at shipyard No.177. She was withdrawn from the fleet on 12 December 1984. During her 16 years of service after returning from Egypt, she took part in a large number of exercises and combat missions, including an exercise in the North Sea in April 1976 together with surface ships and aircraft of the Soviet Navy. After five years of storage in Liepaja, she was sold for disposal in Spain, where she was delivered in December 1989 and subsequently dismantled.

S-3

Submarine *S-180* of Project 613 was laid down on 31 December 1953, at the shipbuilding plant No.112, and launched on 15-16 May 1954. In the spring of 1954, she was transferred to Tallinn to undergo acceptance tests. She was commissioned on 9 December 1954 and on 18 December 1954 she became a part of the IV Fleet. On 22 April 1958, she entered service with the Egyptian Navy as *S-3*. After eight years of service in Egypt, she was returned to the USSR and in the spring of 1968 re-enlisted in the Soviet Baltic Fleet. She was modernised according to the *UTS-613* project and continued to serve as a Training Station *UTS-36* based in Ust-Dvinsk. She was stricken from the fleet on 1 June 1993. On withdrawal of the Russian fleet from Latvia in 1994, she was left in a semi-submerged state, subsequently towed to the port of Riga and scrapped.

S-4

Submarine *S-193* was laid down on 31 March 1954, at the shipbuilding plant No.112, and launched on 14 August 1954. In the autumn of 1954, she was transferred to Leningrad to undergo acceptance tests. The ship was commissioned on 28 April 1955 and on 9 May 1955 she became a part of the IV Fleet. On 22 April 1958, she became part of the Egyptian Navy on lease as *S-4*. After eight

Submarine *S-406* (with two canopies on the wheelhouse) along with other *Whiskey* submarines being dismantled in El Astillero, Spain. (Photo via the archive of A.S. Nikolaev)

years of service in the Egyptian Navy, she was returned to the Soviet Union and in the spring of 1968, she was enlisted in the Soviet Baltic Fleet. She continued service as a Training Station *UTS-37* based in the city of Liepaja. The submarine was stricken from the fleet on 13 September 1993. During the withdrawal of the Russian fleet from Latvia in 1994, she was left in a semi-submerged state in Liepaja, subsequently raised and scrapped.

S-5

Submarine *S-184* of Project 613 was laid down on 23 February 1954, at the shipbuilding plant No.112 and launched on 19 June 1954. In the summer of 1954, she was transferred down the Volga and Caspian Sea to the plant's acceptance base in the city of Baku to undergo acceptance tests. She entered service on 8 December 1954, and on 28 December 1954 was temporarily included in the Caspian Military Flotilla. In the summer of 1955, she was transferred via inland water systems from Baku to the city of Leningrad. On 20 September 1955, she became a part of the IV Fleet. On 24 April 1958, she became a part of the Egyptian Navy on lease as *S-5*. On 14 August 1967, after seven years of service in the Egyptian Navy, she was returned to the USSR. On 24 August 1967 she was re-commissioned in the Soviet Baltic Fleet as *S-15*. In 1968-1970 underwent mid-life repairs. The next repair was in 1978-1980 at SRZ-177 shipyard (Ust-Dvinsk). During the years of service after returning from Egypt, she took part in a large number of exercises and combat missions, including an exercise in the Northeast Atlantic in 1973. She was withdrawn from the fleet on 30 July 1987 and subsequently dismantled at SRZ-177 shipyard in Ust-Dvinsk.

S-6

Submarine *S-228* was laid down on 20 December 1954 at shipyard No.444, launched on 25 June 1955 and entered service on 16 September 1955. Included in the Soviet Black Sea Fleet on 27 September 1955, she was transferred in September 1957 to the Baltic Sea. On 14 October 1957, she was enlisted in the Red Banner Baltic Fleet. In 1958-1960 she underwent a medium repair at the Kronstadt Order of Lenin Marine Plant. She was withdrawn from the Soviet Navy on 19 January 1962 and transferred to Egypt to become the *S-6*. She took part in the wars of 1967 and 1973, and continued serving into the 1990s. It is quite possible that in recent years she was used as a donor of spare parts and for training. During her service, she might have worn pennant numbers 421, 432, 455 or 477.

S-7

Submarine S-226 was laid down on 4 June 1954 at shipyard No.444, launched on 16 March 1955 and entered service on 30 July 1955. Included in the Soviet Black Sea Fleet on 10 August 1955, in autumn 1957 she was transferred within the water communications of the USSR to the Baltic Sea. On 14 October 1957 she was enlisted in the Red Banner Baltic Fleet. Over the years of service in the Baltic Fleet, she underwent modernisation and was based in Kronstadt, Liepaja and Ust-Dvinsk successively. She was withdrawn from the Soviet Navy on 25 December 1965 in connection with the transfer to Egypt. The ship entered the Egyptian Navy as *S-7*. She took part in the wars of 1967 and 1973 and continued serving into the 1990s. It is likely that the last few years of her service she was used as a donor of spare parts and for training. During her service, she might have worn pennant numbers 421, 432, 455 or 477.

S-8

Submarine *S-227* of Project 613 was laid down on 5 August 1954 at shipyard No.444. Launched on 8 October 1954, she entered service on 31 August 1955. The ship was included in the Soviet Black Sea Fleet on 8 September 1955, and in the autumn of 1957, she was transferred within the water communications of USSR to the Baltic Sea. On 14 October 1957 she was enlisted in the Red Banner Baltic Fleet. Was based in Liepaja and Kronstadt. On 7 December 1962, she was withdrawn from the combat fleet, mothballed and in June 1963 put into storage in Kronstadt. She was reactivated in August 1964, and on 1 September 1964 re-enlisted into the Soviet Baltic Fleet, based in Ust-Dvinsk. She was withdrawn from the Soviet Navy on 25 December 1965 in connection with the transfer to Egypt. Entered the Egyptian Navy as *S-8*, took part in the wars of 1967 and 1973, and remained in service into the 1990s. It is quite possible that in recent years she was used as a donor of spare parts and for training. During her service, she might have worn pennant numbers 421, 432, 455 or 477.

Alleged photo of the former submarine *S-19* as a part of the Egyptian Navy in 1958. (Photo via www.deepstorm.ru)

Submarine *S-228* during acceptance tests in 1955. (via collection of V.P. Zablotsky)

415

Submarine *S-280* of Project 613 was laid down on 30 December 1954 at the boathouse of the shipbuilding plant No.112 Krasnoe Sormovo, named after A.A. Zhdanov, in the city of Gorky (nowadays Nizhniy Novgorod). She was launched on 2 June 1954. In June 1955, she was transferred via the USSR internal water communications system to Leningrad to undergo acceptance tests. The ship entered service on 22 September 1955, and on 8 October 1955 she became a part of the VIII Fleet (from 24 December 1955 the Red Banner Baltic Fleet). In December 1960 – January 1961, she moved to Albania to be based at the Pasha Liman naval base. However, due to the breakdown of relations between the USSR and Albania, by May 1961 she had gone back to the Baltic to the naval base in the city of Liepaja. In April 1966, she paid a friendly visit to the port of Oran (Algeria). In 1967, she was in the Mediterranean Sea. In December 1971 – January 1972, she moved from the city of Liepaja to the city of Alexandria for transfer to the Egyptian Navy. She entered service with the Egyptian Navy in January 1972 as *S-28* with pennant number 415 and served during the October 1973 War. She remained in service into the 1990s and might have been used as a donor of spare parts and for training.

Former Soviet submarine *S-280* with pennant number 415 in January 1972 in the port of Alexandria during the transfer to the Egyptian Navy. (via www.deepstorm.ru)

418

Submarine *S-380* of Project 613 was laid down on 19 June 1956, at the boathouse of the shipyard named after. I.I. Nosenko, in the city of Nikolaev. Launched on 29 December 1956, in the spring of 1957, she was transferred to the outfitting base of the plant in the city of Sevastopol to undergo acceptance tests. Commissioned to service on 30 June 1957, on 19 July 1957 the submarine was temporarily included in the Soviet Black Sea Fleet. In August-September 1957, she was transferred using inland water communications systems of the USSR to the White Sea. On 19 September 1957, she was transferred to the Northern Fleet, based in the city of Severodvinsk. In the summer of 1969, after 12 years of service in the Northern Fleet, she was transferred via the White Sea-Baltic Canal to the city of Kronstadt. On 15 August 1969, she became a part of the Soviet Baltic Fleet, based in the city of Paldiski. In December 1971 – January 1972, she moved from the city of Liepaja to the city of Alexandria for transfer to the Egyptian Navy. She entered service with the Egyptian Navy in January 1972 as *S-29* with pennant number 418. As a part of the Egyptian fleet, the last, tenth Egyptian *Whiskey* took part in the October 1973 War. Being the most modern Egyptian submarine of Project 613, the submarine was often captured by photographers.

Lowering the flag from submarine *S-380* in January 1972 by the last Soviet commander of the boat, Captain Nikiforov E.N., when handing over the ship to the Egyptian Navy. (via www.forums.airbase.ru)

Egyptian *Whiskey* with pennant number 418 in 1974. (Dr. David Nicolle Collection)

Egyptian *Whiskey* with pennant number 418 in 1980. (via L&L Van Ginderen)

Raising the Egyptian flag on the former Soviet submarine *S-380* in January 1972. (via www.forums.airbase.ru)

The career of Egyptian Project 613 submarines leaves a mixed impression. On the one hand, their presence in the national navy brought Egypt into the ranks of the strongest Arab fleets and made current and potential adversaries, especially Israel, seriously concerned about their potential capabilities. On the other hand, it is obvious that their great potential was not utilised. If the lack of sunken Israeli ships can still be attributed to a generally small number of potential targets or to outdated Soviet torpedoes, then complete passivity regarding the mining of Israeli coastal waters raises obvious questions. Against the background of the lack of success of the Egyptian *Whiskeys*, the active actions of their peers – the destroyers of the *Skory*-class, which successfully operated as part of the Egyptian fleet during the War of Attrition and the Yom Kippur War – stand out especially.

Another photo of the Egyptian *Whiskey* submarine with pennant number 418. (via www.forums.airbase.ru)

Egyptian *Whiskeys* in 1970s. (via http://forums.airbase.ru)

4

STEADFAST INDONESIAN WHISKEYS

The end of the Second World War radically changed the position of the USSR on the international stage. From a semi-rogue state in the late 1930s, surrounded by numerous hostile countries, in the 1950s the Soviet Union became the world's second military power, with satellite allies in Eastern Europe, and, more importantly, the most attractive political system for those newly emerging countries of the Third World born after the collapse of the colonial order. Many newly independent nations in Asia and Africa looked to the 'communist' Soviet Union as their main ally and ideological leader – or at least for economic assistance and armament. This was how these countries gained access to what the USSR was perhaps most famous for – a variety of weapons systems. As a result, 'rivers' of weapons flowed to Egypt, India, Vietnam, Iraq, Libya and many other countries. However, only a fairly narrow circle of specialists know that the main recipient of Soviet weapons in the late 1950s and early 1960s was Indonesia. For example, the Indonesian Air Force was the first among all the Soviet allies to receive Tupolev Tu-16 bombers (ASCC/NATO reporting name: *Badger*) with KS-1 anti-ship missiles (ASCC/NATO reporting name: *AS-1 Kennel*), which, in the event of an escalation of the conflict with the Netherlands, were to be used against the Dutch aircraft carrier *Karel Doorman*. Jakarta also received various MiG interceptors, Ilyushin Il-28 bombers (ASCC/NATO reporting name: *Beagle*), Mil Mi-4 and Mi-6 helicopters (ASCC/NATO reporting names: *Hound* and *Hook*, respectively), and Antonov An-12 transports (ASCC/NATO reporting name: *Cub*), to name a few. However, by far the largest Indonesian customer for Soviet arms was the local navy. The number of naval weapons supplied to Indonesia could be more than enough to arm any NATO country (with the exception of the USA, Great Britain and France). As part of the 'Towards an Outstanding Fleet Programme' (Indonesian: *'Menuju Angkatan Laut yang Jaya'*), Indonesia received eight Project 30-bis destroyers (ASCC/NATO reporting name: *Skory*-class), a Project 68-bis cruiser *Ordzonikidze* – the only case of export of cruisers in the entire history of the USSR –, 12 Project 183R missile boats (ASCC/NATO reporting name: *Komar*-class), 8 Project 50 patrol vessels (ASCC/NATO reporting name: *Riga*-class), 16 large submarine chasers of Project 122bis (ASCC/NATO reporting name: *Kronshtadt*-class), 14 torpedo boats of Project 183 (ASCC/NATO reporting name: *Bolshevik*-class), 6 Project 254 sea minesweepers (ASCC/NATO reporting name: *T-43*-class), a Project 770 medium landing ship (ASCC/NATO reporting name: *Polnochny*-class), several tankers, a Project 219 degaussing vessel, a Project 310A submarine floating base, a Project 233K floating base, 3 Project 577E medium sea tankers, several tugboats, 18 Project 186 armoured gunboats, 2 torpedo-recovery boats, and more.

Still, by far the most important component in this acquisition was that of twelve Project 613 submarines. Before moving on to a detailed consideration of the career of these vessels, it is important to keep in mind that arms transfers to Indonesia were carried out in within the framework of five open credit lines in the amount of about $1 billion (at preferential interest from 2 to 2.5 percent per annum). A smaller part was paid for by supplies of raw materials. To understand the scale of supplies, one should mind that the purchasing power of US$1 billion in 1960 equalled over US$10 billion in 2023. Most of the warships were supplied at a reduced price, and some were even given for free. For the sake of objectivity, the overwhelming majority of the vessels were 'second-hand', and many were withdrawn from the Soviet Navy due to the Khrushchev's passion for missiles. Not unreasonably, he considered Indonesia as a strategic partner of the USSR in Southeast Asia. The country, a storehouse of natural resources and occupying a strategic position near the most important trade sea routes, was supposed to become a vital element in the global anti-imperialist socialist axis built by the Soviet Union. Khrushchev also maintained cordial relations with Indonesian President Sukarno, and visited Indonesia in 1960. The problem was that Sukarno did not intend to build communism according to Soviet patterns. The system of 'guided democracy' he proclaimed stipulated a predominant role for the state in the economy, the expulsion of Dutch capital and Chinese private business – but it led to an economic collapse by the mid-1960s. For the period 1959-1965 Indonesia's real revenues thus decreased year-on-year by seven times and expenses fell by almost four times, despite the fact that the amount of money in circulation increased from 34.9 to 2,572 billion rupiah. From 1961, Indonesia experienced hyperinflation, the level of which was at least 100 percent. But in the late 1950s, of course, no one could have predicted this.[1]

As in the case of Egypt, a few years before, the first batch of Project 613 submarines were sold to Indonesia via Poland. It is not very clear whom such a 'fig leaf' could deceive, but the Soviet sailors immediately found their own, humorous explanation: the state flags

President Sukarno in Moscow at a meeting with Nikita Khrushchev in 1961. To the sides of the leaders of the two countries are Yuri Gagarin, Soviet cosmonaut, who on 12 April 1961 became the first man to travel into space, and Leonid Brezhnev, who became the new Soviet leader in 1964. (via lenta.ru)

of both Poland and Indonesia consist of two horizontal stripes of white and red. Certainly, Poland has a white stripe at the top and a red one at the bottom, while Indonesia has the opposite – red at the top and white at the bottom. Accordingly, simply turning the flag over solved the problem of replacing it.

On 13 March 1958 an agreement was signed between Poland and Indonesia for the supply of a significant number of warships for the Indonesian Navy – including two Project 613 submarines. The training of Indonesian submarine crews took place in Poland. To ensure their preparation, on 12 September, in Baltiysk, a Special Purpose Expedition-41 (EON-41) was formed under the command of Captain 1st Rank Vladimir Lvovich Gladkov, which included the Project 613 submarine *S-174* under the command of Captain 2nd Rank V. P. Kashirin.

Both Indonesian submarine crews of 112 departed on 5 August 1958 from the port of Surabaya, on board of the Danish vessel *Heinrich Jensen*. The command staff of future submariners consisted of people from aristocratic or wealthy families. For example, Major Raden Panji Poernomo, the future commander of *S-91*, was from an aristocratic family of Indonesian diplomats. Major O.P. Koesno, the future commander of *S-79*, was the owner of drinking establishments in Surabaya, and in his free time, he did not hesitate to stand behind the counter himself selling beer.[2] For submarines, Indonesian sailors were recruited from surface ships and had an understanding of the design of ship mechanisms and equipment. The journey of the future submariners was not easy: by sea to the Yugoslav port of Rijeka, then by train non-stop through Hungary and the Czechoslovakia to Poland. In September 1958, upon arrival in Gdynia, their 9-month study began.

From the beginning of spring 1959, Soviet *Whiskey*-class submarine *S-174* went to sea almost every day to train Indonesian crews under combat training programmes.

The admission of commanders and crews to independent navigation was carried out personally by the Chief of Staff of the Indonesian fleet (the highest post in the Indonesian Navy, effectively the commander of the fleet), Rear Admiral Raditya Soebijakto, who arrived in June 1959 on a visit to Poland.

The examinations of the Indonesian officers and sailors were taken by the officers of the Soviet Navy, led by an admiral.[3] On 16 June 1959, the training of Indonesian crews was completed. Having completed their training, the Indonesian crews departed for their homeland from Poland on 5 August 1959 on the Indonesian Navy transport *Morotai*. However, the commanders of the submarines and some senior officers were transported by train along the Trans-Siberian Railway, in a 9-day trip to Vladivostok, for passage to Indonesia on board of the submarines.[4]

Indonesian sailors in Poland. (Photo via Dispen ALRI)

On 8 August 1959, a detachment of ships consisting of two submarines, *S-79* (commander – Captain 2nd Rank Vladimir Sergeevich Susoev) and *S-91* (Captain 3rd Rank Volovik Fedor Stepanovich), and the tanker *Polyarnik* left the port of Vladivostok for Indonesia. The commander of the detachment was the commander of the cruiser division, Rear Admiral Boris Nikolaevich Lamm, and the chief of staff was Captain 1st Rank Novikov Nikolai Ivanovich. There were several Indonesian officers on board the submarines: on *S-91* there were Major R.P. Poernomo and Captain Sugito, and on *S-79*, Major O.P. Koesno. On 12 August, in the East China Sea,

Indonesian sailors in Poland in 1958. (Albert Grandolini collection)

Admiral Raditya Soebijakto, Chief of Staff of the Indonesian Navy from 1948 to 1959. (Albert Grandolini collection)

tanker *Polyarnik* was replaced by transport *Arkhangelsk*, to which the detachment headquarters moved and all the spare parts and skipper's equipment of the submarines were reloaded. During the entire transition, the boats were monitored by foreign navies.

On 25 August, accompanied by an Indonesian anti-submarine ship, two Soviet submarines entered the outer roadstead of the Surabaya naval base and, a day later, the boats moored in the military harbour. There is no information whether Polish flags were raised on the boats; as far as is known, there were no Polish flags even at the handover ceremony: Soviet flags were lowered. From 4 to 6 September 1959, *S-91* took a test exit to the sea with an Indonesian crew under the command of Major Poernomo.

The day of 12 September 1959 is historic for the Indonesian Navy, since it was on this day that submarines entered service in the national Navy for the first time in history. The Soviet *S-91* received the name RI *Tjakra* and pennant number S-01 (the number was soon changed to 401) and the Soviet *S-79* received the name RI *Nanggala* and pennant number S-02 (changed to 402). The designation RI before the name of a warship was standard in the Indonesian Navy at the time and was an abbreviation for *Republic Indonesia*: this was changed into KRI – for *Kapal Republik Indonesia* (Ship of the Republic of Indonesia). At the ceremony handing over the boats, there were the command of the Indonesian fleet and representatives of the embassies of the USSR and Poland. Admirals and officers of the Indonesian fleet were in ceremonial uniforms with orders and with naval broadswords. Among them was the commander of the Indonesian Navy, Raden Eddy Martadinata.

Major Poernomo was appointed as a commander of RI *Tjakra*, and Major Koesno was appointed as a commander of the submarine RI *Nanggala*.

On the same day, 12 September 1959, a submarine division Divkasel was formed, subsequently reorganised into Skuadron 51 (RON-51), which later transformed into the Submarine Force Command (KDKS). The two submarines, commissioned on 12 September 1959 by decree No. A.4/2/10, formed the Satkalsel Koarmada II Detachment and received the unofficial name Hiu Kencana Corps, which can be translated as Kencana Shark Corps. The Kenkana shark was chosen as a symbol of Indonesian submariners, personifying strength, agility and manoeuvrability. The first commander of the detachment was Major Poernomo, and he also headed the Naval School of Submariners SEKASAL, created on 1 November 1959.

Submarine *S-91* in the Sulawesi Sea on the morning of 21 August 1959, on her way to the Indonesian port of destination. (Albert Grandolini collection)

Above right: The first commanders of the Indonesian submarines, Major Poernomo (to the left) and Major Koesno (to the right), report to the commander of the Indonesian Navy, Colonel Martadinata (backward), during the ceremonial handover of Soviet submarines on 12 September 1959. (Albert Grandolini collection)

Right: Signing of the transfer of the first two *Whiskeys* to the Indonesian Navy on 12 September 1959. (Albert Grandolini collection)

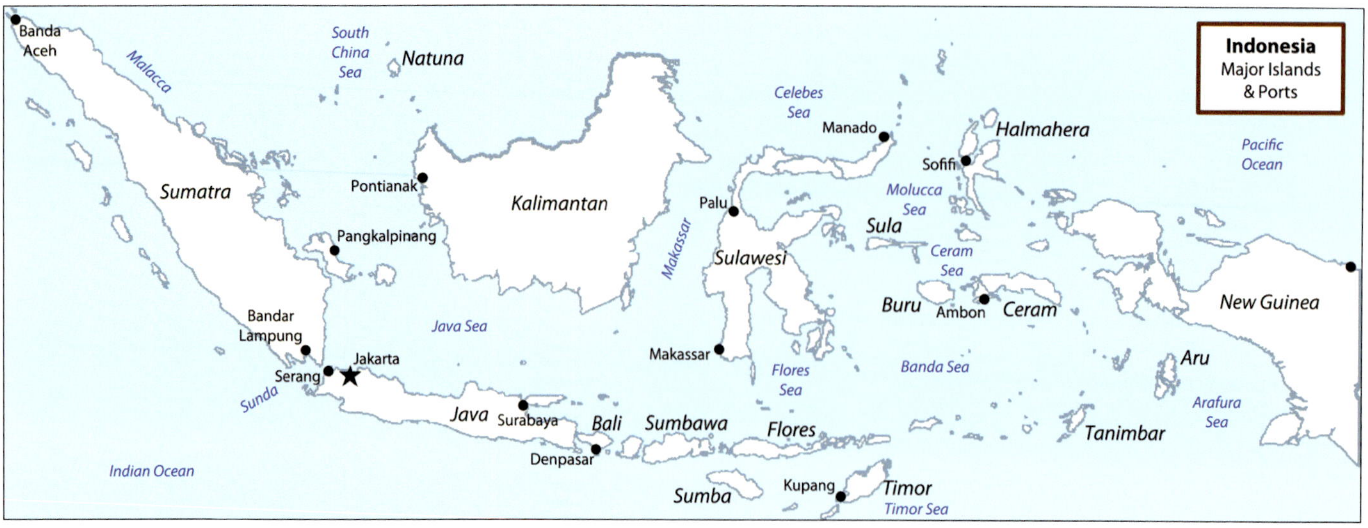

The Indonesian Archipelago with major ports. (b.b.h.illustrations)

As for the Soviet sailors, according to the memoirs of Vladimir Georgievich Lebedko, who served on *S-91*, President Sukarno personally thanked the Soviet personnel during the gala dinner. After the dinner, the Soviet submarine crews boarded the transport *Tobolsk* and sailed back to the USSR.[5]

Speaking about the first two submarines of Project 613 in Indonesia, it is important to note that only these two boats delivered to this country were equipped with automatic double-barrelled 25mm naval artillery mounts 2M-8. They were subsequently dismantled; in the photographs from the early 1960s, both Indonesian *Whiskeys* can be seen equipped with anti-aircraft guns.

In August 1960, during the official visit to Moscow of the Chief of Staff of the Indonesian Navy Rear Admiral R. Martadinat, another round of negotiations took place on the supply of naval equipment to

Former Soviet submarines *S-91* (to the left) and *S-79* (to the right at the pier), September 1959, Surabaya, Indonesia. (Albert Grandolini collection)

Loading torpedoes onto the Project 613 submarine *Nanggala*. (Photo via Jalesveva Jayamahe. 1960. Information Department, Indonesian Navy)

One of the first two Indonesian *Whiskeys*. (Photo via Jalesveva Jayamahe. 1960. Information Department, Indonesian Navy)

Indonesia. The Soviet side agreed to sell the ships on long-term credit at a small interest rate. This was the first agreement on direct supplies of Soviet military equipment, (previously concluded agreements in February 1957 and October 1959 were conditionally defence-related, since they dealt with dual-use equipment) signed at the end of 1960 (in October or November). The amount of the agreement accounted for 283 million US dollars, of which 200 million US dollars were on credit and a discount was provided for 83 million US dollars. The large number of warships intended for delivery included four Project 613 submarines. The submarines were to be repaired and prepared for passage to Indonesia at Plant No.202 in Vladivostok.

At the end of 1960, a directive of the High Command assigned the Soviet Pacific Fleet with the task of training Indonesian crews for Project 613 submarines from May to December 1961. By order of the Commander of the Pacific Fleet, such a boat became *S-235* submarine of the Pacific Fleet. The Indonesian crews had to take a theoretical training course at the 51st Submarine Training Unit of the Pacific Fleet. In January 1961, *S-235* moved from Severnaya Bay of Vladimir Bay to Zolotoy Rog Bay and, during the training of Indonesian crews, became a part of the IV Independent Submarine Brigade of the Pacific Fleet. The vessel was commanded by Captain 3rd Rank Iridiy Aleksandrovich Morozov and senior mate was Captain-Lieutenant Vladimir Serafimovich Lyubimov. The commander of the mine-torpedo unit was Senior Lieutenant Vilen Nikiforovich Pilipenko, and the commander of the torpedo group was Lieutenant Ivan Petrovich Stepanchenko. These torpedo officers bore a large share of responsibility for training torpedo operators and torpedo electricians for Indonesian crews.

The command of the Pacific Fleet assigned the submarine the following task: within three months (February – April 1961) to prepare the ship for accepting Indonesian crews on board one by one for their practical training. From May to December 1961, on *S-235*, Indonesian crews had to undergo practical training in the first and second tasks of the combat training course. According to the orders received from the Pacific Fleet headquarters, the Khrom-KM radar identification system was dismantled on the submarine, the Nakat-M search radar was replaced with the Anker radar, the technical documentation was corrected, torpedoes 53-39PM, SAET-60 and SAET-50M were unloaded, with 53-39 and SAET-50 torpedoes loaded instead.[6] It is interesting to note here that Alexander Rozin writes that SAET-50 guided torpedoes were delivered during the transfer of the mentioned four submarines, while at the same time the author came across statements from Indonesian sources that these torpedoes were delivered only with the next (third) batch of Soviet submarines.

Note that despite the great pride in modern Indonesian sources that the country's fleet received guided torpedoes back in the early 1960s, the quality of the torpedoes was very controversial. According to the memoirs of A.V. Batarshev:

Tjakra submarine equipped with a 2M-8 anti-aircraft gun. *Tjakra* can be distinguished from *Nanggala* by the presence of a front wheelhouse door. (Albert Grandolini collection)

The torpedoes specialists also had to deal with SAET-50 electric torpedoes. Under conditions of high temperatures and long-term storage in torpedo tubes, their acoustic equipment reduced its characteristics, as mentioned above. Practical firing at the training site (northwest of Madura Island, 80 miles north of Surabaya) with these torpedoes showed their inconsistency in tropical conditions. The torpedoes were not aimed at the target. Flagmin A. Batarshev compiled a detailed report on this, which was transmitted to the command. Upon returning to the Soviet Union, already in May 1963, he additionally reported this precedent to the Main Mine and Torpedo Directorate of the Navy in Moscow.[7]

One of the first exits of an Indonesian *Whiskey* into the sea. (Photo via Jalesveva Jayamahe. 1960. Information Department, Indonesian Navy)

SAET-50 torpedo in one of the Indonesian museums. (Albert Grandolini collection)

On 25 March 1961, a detachment of selected Indonesian sailors, led by Major A.T. Wingjoprajitno, left Indonesia for nine months training in the Soviet Union. In April 1961, 400 Indonesian sailors arrived in Vladivostok for training. Notably, all Indonesian officers, without exception, came from wealthy or aristocratic families. Previously, they studied at naval schools in England, the Netherlands and the USA and spoke very good English. Non-commissioned- and other ranks were mainly formed from poor families. Indonesian submariners conscientiously performed their duties, both non-commissioned officers and privates unquestioningly followed the orders and instructions of their commanders and superiors. As planned, practical training of Indonesian crews on *S-235* began in mid-April 1961.

However, none of the Indonesian officers, let alone sergeants and sailors, spoke Russian. Therefore, several dozen Soviet translators were involved in the preparation, but only three of them had knowledge of the Indonesian language, the rest spoke only English. But the sailors, unlike the officers, did not speak English, and since they were the bulk of them, the main burden fell on three translators who spoke Indonesian.

The main emphasis in the practical training of Indonesian crews on *S-235* was made on the technical side: competent operation of weapons and technical equipment, correct execution of commands, detailed study of the material part of their management, error-free actions during inspection and testing of weapons and technical equipment (turning mechanisms). The above activities constitute the most important elements of the first task of the Combat Training course. The success of the submarine's accident-free navigation during the training of task two of the Combat Training Course largely depends on their high-quality implementation. To assist in the practical training of Indonesian submariners, one translator was assigned to each of their crews (sometimes, although rarely, two translators), who duplicated the commands in Indonesian via the ship's radio broadcast installation Kashtan, giving appropriate explanations and advice. The training programme for each of the Indonesian crews provided for the full completion of the first two tasks of the combat training course. Indonesian submariners acquired initial skills in submarine navigation on the surface and underwater. They independently carried out trimming of the submarine, her diving (except for emergency dives) and ascent, and bubble-less torpedoes shooting. After completing each of the tasks, the level of training of the Indonesian crews was checked and assessed by the headquarters of the 4th Separate Brigade of Submarines, with a subsequent report on the results of the inspection to the headquarters of the Pacific Fleet. All Indonesian crews were trained in the scope of the first and second tasks of the Combat Training Course within the planned time frame and passed them with a 'good' rating. On 12 January 1962, the crews of Indonesian submariners returned to their homeland.

On 31 December 1961, four submarines of Project 613 left Vladivostok for Indonesia. These were *S-218* (Captain 2nd Rank A.V. Koltsov), *S-219* (Captain 3rd Rank G.G. Kostev), *S-223* (Captain Andreev), and *S-225* (Captain 2nd Rank Yu .M. Dzhanelidze). The boats moved on the surface. Abeam the island of Okinawa, their silhouettes were seen from a merchant ship, and thirty minutes later American Neptune patrol planes appeared above them. From that moment on, aircraft 'led' the boats to the Makassar Strait. On 15 January 1962, the submarines arrived in Surabaya, accompanied by a mother ship. On 29 January, the submarines were transferred to the Indonesian Navy and received the following names:

- RI *Nagabanda* (pennant number 403, Major A.T. Wingjoprajitno),
- RI *Trisula* (pennant number 404, Major Teddy Asikin Natanegara),
- RI *Nagarangsang* (pennant number 405, Major Agus Subroto), and
- RI *Tjandrasa* (also '*Chandrasa*', pennant number 406, Major Mas Mardiono).[8]

By mid-February, most of the Soviet crews returned to Vladivostok, though the instructors remained. The last 20 sailors from the four transferred submarines left for Surabaya on 19 June 1962, from there on the morning of the 20th they left for Jakarta, and from there by Aeroflot plane to Moscow.

The next delivery of Project 613 submarines to Indonesia was associated with the aggravation of the situation around West Irian, where there were already direct clashes between the Netherlands and Indonesia. On 2 May 1962, Indonesian Foreign Minister Subandrio went to Moscow, where he held negotiations from 3 to 9 May. On 4 May, the Indonesian government delegation was received in the

Indonesian sailors of one of the Project 613 submarines transferred from the USSR. (Albert Grandolini collection)

Kremlin by Deputy Chairman of the Council of Ministers of the USSR A. Kosygin. Soviet-Indonesian negotiations ended with the participation of the Soviet Foreign Minister A.A. Gromyko, the Soviet Minister of Defense R. Ya. Malinovsky and other officials. On 8 May 1962, the fifth agreement was concluded on the supply of arms in the amount, according to American data, of 95 million US dollars, of which 69 million US dollars were provided on credit, and a discount was provided for 26 million US dollars. Delivery was planned three months after signing the agreement. It was then that the Soviet leadership granted the request of the Indonesians to send their submariners and pilots to Indonesia with their possible participation in the battles to liberate West Irian. A more complete picture of how this was agreed in Moscow can be found in the statements of N.S. Khrushchev and Anastas Mikoyan. In a conversation with the Romanian communist leaders in October 1962, Khrushchev said that Sukarno, taking the initiative, sent Subandrio to Moscow to ask for 'submarines, planes and crews for these things.' Mikoyan said roughly the same thing to Soviet officers in November 1962: 'This summer, when Sukarno was preparing to solve this problem…we gave him several submarines with Soviet crews, several (I cannot quote the number) Tu-16s with those designed to destroy ships with missiles, so that they could destroy the Dutch ships.'

In 1962, the number of Soviet Army and Navy personnel who arrived in the Indonesian Republic increased to 1,740. On 4 May, it was announced that the 54th Separate Submarine Brigade would be created from the ships of the VI submarine squadron. The brigade included submarines *S-235*, *S-236*, *S-239* and the floating base *Ayakhta* from the 126th Submarine Brigade, submarines *S-290*, *S-292* from the 19th Submarine Brigade, and *S-391* from the 124th Submarine Brigade. The command, headquarters and political department of the brigade were staffed mainly by personnel from the 126th Submarine Brigade. Rear Admiral Anatoly Antonovich Rulyuk was appointed commander of the 54th Independent Submarine Brigade.

During training on submarines, modern equipment and weapons were removed from the submarines and export simplified versions were installed, which reduced the combat effectiveness of the submarines. For example, low-noise propellers were removed and replaced with old ones, and more outdated torpedoes 53-39 and SAET-50 were also provided.

On 25 May 1962, *S-236* (Captain 2nd Rank Dvornikov Yuri Vladimirovich) and *S-292* (Captain 2nd Rank Targonin Grigory Valentinovich) under the command of Chief of the Staff of 54th Independent Submarine Brigade (Captain 1st Rank Fedor Diomidovich Grishelev, embarked on board *S-236*), went out to sea and headed towards Indonesia. According to a British intelligence report, on 28 May two Indonesia-linked submarines were spotted off the coast of Taiwan, heading south. On 7 June, having completed a 15-day journey, they arrived in Surabaya. The boats were met at the port by an Indonesian submarine, on the bridge of which was Captain 2nd Rank Yuri Dzhanelidze. On 2 June 1962, the second detachment of the 54th Independent Submarine Brigade left for Indonesia – four *Whiskey*-class submarines: *S-235* (Captain 3rd Rank Shvanderov Yuri Grigorievich), *S-391* (Captain 2nd Rank Antipov Anatoly Nikolaevich), *S-239* (Captain 2nd Rank Potapov Petr Aleksandrovich), *S-290* (Captain 2nd Rank Kodes Alexander Aleksandrovich), and the floating base *Ayakhta* (Captain Voronov Mikhail Panteleevich). The brigade commander, Rear Admiral A.A. Rulyuk, together with his headquarters, sailed on the floating base *Ayakhta,* which also carried the personnel of mine-torpedo units (Lieutenant Ivan Stepanchenko), 75 percent of whom were from teams of coastal bases of different submarine brigades of the Soviet Pacific Fleet. The preparation of torpedoes 53-39 and SAET-50, and their repair in the conditions of a coastal base were entrusted to these highly experienced torpedo weapons specialists.

The first two days of the transition were relatively calm. Sea of Japan waves were within 1-2 points, visibility was good. Starting from the third day of the passage, American and Japanese Lockheed P2V Neptune patrol aircraft, as well as Martin P5M Merlin anti-submarine flying boats, began to fly over the mother ship and boats. The air escort of the brigade's ships continued day and night until they entered the Sulawesi Sea. On 25 June, at the pier of the main naval base of Surabaya, the sailors were met by the chief military adviser in Indonesia, Rear Admiral Grigory Korneevich Chernobay. Rear Admiral Anatoly Antonovich Ruluk reported to him the arrival of the brigade in Surabaya, about the condition of the ships' equipment and about the morale of the personnel.

With the arrival of the second group of ships of the 54th Independent Submarine Brigade detachment in Surabaya, all Project 613 boats with Soviet crews (six units) were consolidated into the 50th Operational Submarine Brigade. The floating base

President Sukarno skilfully used his good personal relationship with Nikita Khrushchev to obtain modern Soviet weapons systems on preferential terms. (Albert Grandolini collection)

Ayakhta, with the headquarters and political department, moved to a separate pier located one and a half kilometres from the piers where Soviet boats were moored. On the second day of their stay in Surabaya, all submariners were dressed in Indonesian uniforms, but without insignia.

Operation Jayawijaya

By this time, six Soviet submarines had already been considered in the developed plan for Operation Jayawijaya – a joint attack on the island of Biak, which was under Dutch control. According to the plan, 12 submarines and 20 Tu-16 and Tu-16KS bombers were to become involved. At the same time, six submarines were with Soviet crews, and out of 20 bombers, more than half were also flown by Soviet pilots, since the Indonesians did not have time to train the required number.[9]

The action plan for Operation Jayawijaya was developed on 18 May 1962, with a planned start on 12 August. The operation was divided into several stages with the participation of strike aircraft, navy and landing forces (8,100 soldiers – 6,700 paratroopers and 1,400 army infantry).

The Navy operated more than 70 combat and amphibious ships, including four Project 613 submarines: *Nagabanda, Tjandrasa, Nagarangsang* and *Trisula*. On 7 July 1962, the submarines left Surabaya and by 9 July they were already operating in the prescribed area (notably, *Nanggala* and *Tiakra* were not involved). The purpose of the deployment was to gain advantage at sea in preparation for amphibious operations. During Operation Tjakra (20-29 July), the submarines were deployed at the following positions: *Nagabanda* between Manokwari and Biak Island, *Trisula* between Biak Island and Japen, *Tjandrasa* between the island of Numfor and Manokwari, and *Nagarangsang* near Sorong.

On 17 July, the deployment of the landing Operation Jayawijaya began. As part of it, Operation Dolphin ('Lumba-Lumba') was carried out to land special forces detachments from three submarines – *Tjandrasa* (Major Mas Mardiono), *Nagarangsang* (Major Agoes Subroto), and *Trisula* (Major Teddy Asikin Natanegara). The landing of the special forces detachments (each of the boats taken carried 15) was to take place in Tanah Merah Bay on a hidden beach near Kotabaru, West Irian.[10] The special forces commander, Senior Lieutenant Lettu Dolf, (according to other sources his name was Dolf Latumahina), stood on board of *Trisula*. The task was quite difficult, as the waters en route to the target were patrolled by Dutch warships, which were able to detect the Indonesian submarines as they entered the waters of Galvin Bay. The discovered submarines were attacked by depth charges. As a result of the attacks, *Nagarangsang* suffered damage to her vertical stabiliser and was forced to return to base. But *Tjandrasa* and *Trisula* continued the mission. As they approached the target, both boats rose to periscope depth to clarify the situation and discovered heavy fog on the surface of the sea that made it impossible to detect enemy ships. Believing that there were no enemy ships around, the *Trisula*'s commander ordered to surface. To their shock, the Indonesian sailors discovered a Dutch submarine on a parallel course, and a Neptune patrol aircraft in the air. All this caused the Indonesian submarine to quickly dive, especially since the Dutch patrol ships began firing flare shells to detect submarines. Given the presence of Dutch ships in the area of a potential landing site, the commander of *Trisula* decided to cancel the landing. Special forces commander Lettu Dolf did not agree with this decision and suggested going farther east and landing in the Jayapura area (Indian Jayapura). However, the submarine commander found the coast near Jaipur too well defended and cancelled the mission, ordering a return to base. There is another version of *Trisula*'s participation in this operation. According to the recollections of the famous Indonesian submariner and retired admiral Handogo, the submarine launched two rubber boats and successfully landed troops, but seeing suspicious lights on the shore that consistently blinked and went out, Major Teddy Asikin Natanegara recalled the special forces team to the submarine. Just at this moment, *Trisula* was discovered by a Dutch patrol plane and a destroyer, which forced the boat to urgently dive to a depth of 150 metres, and then 180 metres. This was done to avoid enemy sonar and depth charges. *Trisula* eventually returned to base at Kupa-Kupa on Halmahera Island.[11]

In either case, the only remaining submarine, *Tjandrasa*, continued the mission. Rising to the surface at night, the submarine launched a rubber boat for the landing of special forces. However, due to the appearance of a Dutch patrol plane in the air, it was forced to dive again. After some time *Tjandrasa* rose to the surface again and to surprise of her crew, found the rubber boat still nearby. This

The Mandala Command for the Liberation of West Irian (Indonesian: Komando Mandala Pembebasan Irian Barat) inspects one of the Indonesian submarines in the summer of 1962. Judging by the presence of the 2M-8 anti-aircraft gun, this is one of two submarines delivered in 1959. (Albert Grandolini collection)

was collected and the submarine dived and began to wait for the next night. This time, the action passed much more calmly, no Dutch ships or planes were observed, and the special forces were safely landed on the shore. Upon returning to base, all *Tjandrasa* crew members were awarded the highest award, the Sacred Star ('Bintang Sakti'). This was the only time in the history of the Indonesian Navy that this order was awarded to submarine crew.

Final preparations for Operation Jayawijaya began with the movement of troops from locations in Jakarta, Surabaya and Amahaya. The Indonesian fleet assembled in the waters around the Banggai Islands on the east coast of Sulawesi, Peling Bay and Bangkalan Bay. The Indonesians planned to carry out the first air attacks on Dutch targets on 10 August. On 12 August the attack on Biak Island was to begin.

President Sukarno receives the Submariner's Badge (Indonesian: Brevet Hiu Kencana) from the Commander-in-Chief of the Indonesian Navy Submarine Force, Commodore Abdulkadir Manambai in a ceremony held on the deck of a Project 613 submarine in 1962. The presence of the 2M-8 anti-aircraft gun again indicates that this is one of two submarines delivered in 1959. (Albert Grandolini collection)

The situation was heating up by the hour. US President Kennedy, at a meeting with Indonesian Foreign Minister Subandrio, said that he knew that the submarines of the Indonesian Navy were manned by Soviet sailors and, as a result, would have to take the Dutch side if Indonesia invaded Western New Guinea. Fortunately, on 15 August 1962, Subandrio and the Dutch delegation reached an agreement that Western New Guinea would be transferred to Indonesia on 1 May 1963 and, as a consequence, the conflict was resolved. Of course, despite Kennedy's warning, the Indonesians maintained military pressure on the Dutch until the completion of negotiations. Soviet submariners were also involved.

Soviet Involvement

Back in mid-July 1962, the commander of the Indonesian Navy, Admiral Martadinata, met with the senior officer of Soviet military specialists in Indonesia, Rear Admiral G.K. Chernobay, and informed him about the upcoming operation and the use of Soviet submariners in it. After meeting with the Indonesian fleet commander, Admiral Chernobay went to the Soviet Ambassador N.A. Mikhailov and reported the conversation to him. As a result, coded messages were sent to Moscow to the ministers of foreign affairs and defence with two signatures. Two or three days later, a response came from the Ministry of Defence in Moscow:

> Higher authorities allowed the crews of six submarines as a part of the Indonesian Navy to take part in hostilities. A. Grechko.

On 20 July, Rear Admiral G.K. Chernobay, the naval attaché in Indonesia, Captain 1st Rank Bondarenko, and the Soviet Ambassador to Indonesia N.A. Mikhailov arrived from Jakarta at the naval base in Surabaya to Soviet submariners. They had a conversation with the brigade commander and the head of the political department, where they informed them about the participation of Soviet sailors in the upcoming operation.

In late July, about a week before entering the patrol areas, the brigade commander, Rear Admiral Anatoly Ruluk, conducted a group exercise with the boat commanders. In addition to the commanders, the chief of staff Fyodor Grishelev, deputy brigade commander Valentin Sinelnikov and head of the political department Alexander Kamenev were allowed to participate in the group exercise. On a large-scale marine chart off the northwestern coast of the island New Guinea were designated six rectangular positions 20×40 miles. The farthest of them, the eastern one, was intended for *S-236*, and the closest one, the western one, was for *S-292*. In accordance with this, *S-236* was to go out first, and *S-292* was the last.

The transition to positions was divided into two stages. The first was a surface passage without stealth to a refuelling point in the port of Bitung, located in the north-eastern tip of the island of Sulawesi. The second must be carried out by boats independently and secretly: during daylight hours they had to go underwater, bypassing the island of Morotai, the northernmost island of the Moluccas archipelago, from the north. During the group exercise, commanders developed and reported their decisions on transition and manoeuvring at patrol positions. The main problem was the lack of accurate data on the location and forces of the potential enemy.

The first to go on the expedition was *S-236* (Captain 2nd Rank Yu. Dvornikov), on 28 July; the second, *S-235*, went to sea on the same day (Captain 3rd Rank Yu. Shvanderov). A day later, *S-290* (Captain 2nd Rank A. Kodes), *S-239* (Captain 2nd Rank P. Protasov), and *S-391* (Captain 2nd Rank A. Antipov) went out to the sea. The sixth boat, *S-292* (Captain 2nd Rank G. Targolin) was the last to leave the port of Surabaya on the morning of 30 July. Each boat had several Indonesian sailors on board, including a navigator, an interpreter, a radiotelegraph operator and a steering signalman.

After the Soviet submarines left, the floating base *Ayakhta* with the headquarters and political department on board was transferred from Surabaya to Jakarta to manage them. Lines of communication were established with the operational command of the operation, as well as with the headquarters of the Navy and Air Force.

Replenishment of diesel fuel and oil reserves to full standards was planned at the port of Bitung. However, the arrival of the tanker with fuel and lubricants at the port was delayed. The brigade commander made the decision not to deviate from the schedule for the boats to patrol positions, to refuel the boats with diesel fuel and oil to full standards in the port of Bitung in a chain: each subsequent boat transferred fuel and lubricants to the previous one to full standards, until a special tanker arrived at the port for this purpose. And so, it happened. The task of refuelling the submarines with fuel and oil was completed successfully, and the schedule for the submarines to enter patrol positions was not violated. However, we note that only five submarines were refuelled in this way, and the sixth, *S-292*, was refuelled from the Indonesian floating base *Bengawan* that came with the Indonesian brigade to Butung. A few hours after taking fuel and lubricants to full capacity, *S-292* submarine was about to enter a patrol position when, unexpectedly, a circular RDO came through about postponing the operation. The boat remained in Bitung, waiting for the rest of the brigade's boats to return there.

The remaining submarines were in position at sea. As they moved away from Butung Island, coastal landmarks gradually disappeared along the route. There were no radio beacons or navigation systems 'Loran-A' and 'Loran-S' along the route. The only possibility for determining the location was the starry sky during the evening and morning navigational twilight. In the absence of targets (signals), the boat briefly floated to a positional standing. The astronomical crew was called to the navigation bridge, measured the heights of the stars with sextants to determine the position lines and subsequently determine the location of the submarine in the sea. Astronomical calculations were well prepared. The discrepancy between the average position of the submarines did not exceed 1.5-2 miles, which is considered a good indicator for determining the position of a ship at sea in the sailing conditions that existed at that time in the Java Sea and the Banda Sea. During the period of combat patrol, as well as during the transition to the area, no ships, vessels and aircraft were visually detected, and no radar signals were detected.

The order to cancel the operation was unexpected and, at the same time, long-awaited by everyone. Retired captain 1st rank Rudolf Viktorovich Ryzhikov then first mate of *S-236* recalled:

> Less than a day remained until the time of 'H' (the start of unlimited submarine warfare). The area is empty for now. Apart from the noise of schools of fish, the acousticians heard nothing. Suddenly…in the next communication session we received a 'radio'. The commander locked himself and the cryptographer in his cabin. What's in the encryption? The cabin door opened with a bang. The commander ordered the officers to gather and invited Indonesian officers to the wardroom. Very seriously (but I saw from subtle signs that he was happy) the commander read the encryption. 'Commanders pl pl…Upon receipt of this, surface. Return to Bitung on the surface. In Bitung, wait for further orders without reducing combat readiness. The issue of liberating West Irian can be resolved peacefully. Commander-in-Chief of the Navy.'

The first to return to the port of Bitung was *S-391*. After some time, the rest of the brigade's boats arrived, the last of which was *S-236*, whose patrol position was the farthest – on the northeastern approaches to West Irian. The senior group of boats, deputy brigade commander, Captain 1st Rank Sinelnikov, ordered all boats, without reducing their 6-hour readiness, to carry out monthly maintenance and repair work, inter-trip inspection and preventative repair of weapons and technical equipment.

On the morning of 20 August, the submariners received an encrypted message: 'The issue of transferring West Irian to Indonesia has been resolved peacefully.' The *S-236* left for Surabaya, followed by the rest at intervals of six to eight hours; the *S-292* was the last to leave Bitung Bay.

For the 50th Operational Submarine Brigade the Operation Alugoro was successfully completed. Upon returning to Surabaya, the brigade retained the designation the 54th Independent Submarine Brigade of the Pacific Fleet. At the naval base of Surabaya, the brigade commander, Rear Admiral Anatoly Antonovich Rulyuk, gathered boat commanders and staff officers, collecting their brief reports on the results of the military campaign off the West Irian, as well as reports from flagship specialists on the actions of personnel during the campaign. On 30 August, Rear Admiral Grigory Chernobay arrived from Jakarta to the military camp. After a preliminary conversation with the brigade commander, Grigory Korneevich met with the submariners directly in Kapala. Having heard the boat commanders the admiral noted that the General Headquarters of the Navy assessed the actions of the boat brigade overall positively, and thanked the submariners for the high-quality implementation of the tasks set by the headquarters.

Lessons Learned

On 3 September 1962, the brigade commander summed up the final results of completing the tasks of the military campaign. Two further main tasks were set:

1. Training of Indonesian crews for our boats with delivery of the first two stages of the Combat Training course within three months.
2. Transfer of submarines to the Indonesian side.

Completing the first main task was fraught with certain difficulties. They consisted in the fact that the Indonesian crews, who were to replace the personnel of six boats, were not trained at the Training Centre near Vladivostok (on the Russian Island). The same Indonesian sailors who previously trained on Russian Island were mainly assigned to boats previously delivered to the Indonesian Navy.

For the subsequent delivery of submarines, the Indonesian side had to begin dock repairs in the near future, without slowing down the pace of training of crews. By mid-September, *S-236* and *S-292* began docking. The boat commanders and the command of the brigade were informed that the repair work would be carried out exclusively by the workers of the ship repair enterprises. The crews of the boats were assigned only the tasks of monitoring and accepting docking work. Two weeks were allotted for dock repairs: upon completion of the work, *S-236* and *S-292* left the dock, their place was taken by the next two submarines. By mid-October, all the brigade's boats had undergone dock repair work. In parallel with this, the training and testing of Indonesian crews continued.

Against this background, the Soviet submariners completed the transfer of six vessels. Theoretical classes with Indonesian crews and practicing elements of Stage 1 (Organisation of service and preparation of submarines for sailing) of the Submarine Combat Training Course were carried out intensively in November and the first half of December 1962. Once all six boats were ready, the command of the Indonesian brigade involved both Indonesian and Soviet flagship specialists. The boats then went to the training ground north of Bawean Island to test their manoeuvrable elements on the surface. Diesel engines were tested at full speed. Grigory Targonin's boat, *S-292*, at 500rpm showed a speed of 18.2 knots, but the rest of the boats could not reach 17 knots.

Submarine Tender

It is worth noting that in addition to the transfer of the submarines, the Soviet Union also transferred support vessels for the operation of the Indonesian submarine fleet. In spring of 1962, a new ship of Project 310A (ASCC/NATO reporting name: *Don*-class) – the floating base of submarines *Nikolai Kartashov* (pennant number 441) – rolled off the slipways of shipyard No.198, in Nikolaev: it was intended for the Indonesian Navy. The ship's crew comprised 18 officers and 402 other ranks. On 31 May 1962, the ship was accepted into the Soviet Navy, and on 2 July 1962, she set sail for the port of Surabaya, commanded by Captain 2nd Rank Vladimir

Varfolomeevich Verteev. His Indonesian backup was Major Sudirman. There were 840 sailors on board – 420 Soviet and 420 Indonesian. After a long and rather difficult journey (the ship was caught in a six-day storm in the Indian Ocean), *Nikolai Kartashov* arrived in Indonesia on 29 July. On 10 August 1962, in Surabaya, a ceremony was held to transfer her to Indonesian Navy, which renamed the vessel to *Ratulangi*. Commanded by Major Sudirman, the ship then headed to the area of Bawean Island to conduct a combat exercise with artillery firing on the bare island of Gundul. Captain 2nd Rank Verteev was at the bridge as a commander's instructor. The shooting was successful, and, feeling confident, Major Sudirman refused further help from the Soviet sailors.

Ratulangi, in addition to her intense and long-term service in the Indonesian Navy, was especially interesting for two reasons. The first were constant changes of pennant numbers. Initially, she received a four-digit number 4101. This was soon changed to 400, then to 440, 552, 901, and 301. The second point, little known even to Russian readers, is the participation of *Ratulangi* during the Indonesian occupation of East Timor in 1975. The submarine tender armed with solid artillery weapons (four single-barrel 100mm artillery mounts B-34USMA and four 57mm twin mounts ZIF-31) was a part of the Indonesian squadron transporting marines, PT-76 amphibious tanks and BTR-50 amphibious armoured personnel carriers. *Ratulangi* even took part in a 'demonstrative' shelling of the shore with her 57mm guns.[12]

Returning to the events of 1962, once back to their base in Surabaya, on 15 December 1962, all six Soviet submarines of Project 613 – *S-235*, *S-236*, *S-239*, *S-290*, *S-292* and *S-391* – were transferred to the Indonesians. The submarines received the following names:

- RI *Alugoro*, (pennant number 407, Captain S.F. Makalew),
- RI *Tjundamani*, (pennant number 408, Captain R.D. Sudiono),
- RI *Widjajadanu*, (pennant number 409, Major Assyr Mochtar),
- RI *Pasopati*, (pennant number 410, Captain Sigitjoto Sudirdjo),
- RI *Hendradjala*, (pennant number 411, Captain R.M. Khandogo), and
- RI *Bramasta*, (pennant number 412, Captain Leo Darsa).

Sadly, it remains unknown which submarine received which of the names: Indonesian sources usually quote *Widjajadanu* as the former S-239, but otherwise they frequently confuse their pennant numbers. In the A.V. Batarshev and V.S. Lyubimov's book, *The Six Hundred and Thirteenth in Indonesia*, *S-236* is noted as becoming *Bramastra*, and *S-292* the *Alugoro*.

Simultaneously with the submarines, on 15 December 1962, the Soviet Pacific Fleet floating base Project 233K *Ayakhta* was transferred to the Indonesian Navy. She received the name RI *Thamrin* and pennant number 4102 (later changed to 902).

As for the Soviet crews of the transferred submarines, the rank and file, political officers and doctors set off on the passenger ship *Vladivostok* back to the USSR on 28 December 1962. At the same time, most of the officers remained in Surabaya for further training of Indonesian submariners. Most of them went home in February-March 1963.

The newly transferred submarines with Indonesian crews soon began to go to sea. For example, in April 1963, as part of Operation VISHNU MUKTI, *Tjundamani* and *Alugoro*, together with *Nagarangsang*, carried out a 'show of force' off the coast of Western Guinea.

On 25 March 1963, the Minister of Defence of the USSR, Marshal Malinovsky, arrived in Indonesia on a visit. He held meetings with President Sukarno, the command of the army, air force and navy. On 27 March, at a ceremony at Merdeka Palace, Marshal Malinowski said that the Soviet Union, through its massive military aid to Indonesia, had dealt a blow to Dutch colonialism in Southeast Asia. On 28 March, he observed the Operation Sea Eagle manoeuvres of aviation and navy in the Java Sea, which involved destroyers, combat boats, submarines and Il-28 bombers. In early April, he completed his Indonesian visit by flying to Burma.

Perhaps the most famous photograph of the submarine tender *Ratulangi*. Next to her there are several *Whiskey* submarines. (Albert Grandolini collection)

Future commander of *Bramasta*, Leo Darsa (fourth from the left) among 15 young Indonesian cadets who trained in the Netherlands at the Royal Naval College (Dutch: Koninklijk Instituut voor de Marine) in Den Helder. The photo was taken in Jakarta in 1952. (*Dan toch maar!*)

Whiskey submarines of the Indonesian Navy: *Bramasta*, pennant number 412 and *Tjundamani*, pennant number 408. (satselhiukencana)

Floating submarine base of the Indonesian Navy *Thamrin*. (Author's collection)

In 1963-1964, a number of Soviet military and civilian specialists were sent to Indonesia to organise repairs and restore the combat readiness of submarines. In particular, among those who were sent to Indonesia there were the commander of mine-torpedo unit of nuclear submarine *K-8* of the Northern Fleet, 1957-1963, Captain 3rd Rank Erin Nikita Fomich, and ship designer Alexey Ignatievich, who was engaged in the repairs of submarines in Bolshoy Kamen (Primorye) in the early 1960s.

In 1964, a small group of Soviet submariners based in Surabaya, a kind of guarantee team, managed to repair one of the previously transferred submarines. They and the Indonesian crew went to the outer roadstead on the repaired boat, dove and surfaced, moving back and forth both on the surface and underwater.

Except for a short stand-off with Malaysia, lasting from 1 October 1963 to 2 February 1964, Indonesia's primary issues were with the countries of the British Commonwealth. In August-September 1964, the Indonesian fleet found itself at the forefront of a confrontation with the Royal Navy. In August, the British announced their intention to exercise the right of the free passage through the Indonesian straits. On 27 August, they carried out a 'show of force' by sending the aircraft carrier HMS *Victorious* (R38) – escorted by destroyers HMS *Cavendish* (R15) and HMS *Caesar* (R07) – from Singapore, through the Sunda Straits, to Australia. Considering this an act of war, on 2 September, Indonesian Foreign Minister Subandrio issued a stark ultimatum to the Royal Navy, not to attempt passing the Sunda Strait without permission. The Indonesian Navy (Tentara Nasional Indonesia Angkatan Laut; TNI-AL) immediately began large-scale military exercises in the Sunda Strait to demonstrate the seriousness of the ultimatum. A naval group was deployed in the Sunda Strait area including the *Sverdlov*-class cruiser *Irian*, *Skory*-class destroyers *Brawidjaja* and *Diponegoro*, and the *Riga*-class frigate *Jos Sudarso*. In addition, as a part of Operation KENTJANA, the Indonesians deployed four Project 613 submarines to the straits: *Pasopati* and *Tjandrasa* nearby, *Alugoro* and *Tjundamani* near the Lombok Strait.

Initially sailing from Fremantle, Australia, the Royal Navy's task force headed north-northwest towards the Sunda Strait. South of Java, it was reinforced by the HMS *Hampshire* (D06), and frigates HMS *Dido* (F104) and HMS *Berwick* (F115), and on 12 September the entire force passed through the Lombok Strait (between the islands of Bali and Lombok), asserting its continued right of unimpeded passage in international waters. While the Indonesians decided not to start a war, the skipper of the submarine RI *Alugoro* decided to mark the presence of his vessel and the Indonesian Navy. According to Indonesian data, the submarine was not detected by the British anti-submarine forces until she surfaced, and her appearance was a shock to the British sailors. After signalling, 'Have a nice voyage', and receiving the response, 'Thank you, the same to you', the boat went its own way, while the Royal Navy's task force turned west for Singapore.

One of the most interesting episodes of the service of Project 613 boats in the Indonesian Navy was their unaccomplished participation in the Indo-Pakistan War of 1965. With the outbreak of this conflict, President Sukarno promised assistance to Pakistan. For example, after the outbreak of the conflict, the commander of the Indonesian Navy, Admiral Martadinata, offered to help the Pakistanis to capture the Andaman and Nicobar Islands, located in relative proximity to Sumatra (possibly in order to annex them in the future). On 17 October 1965, the Task Force X was established, including two *Komar*-class missile boats, four torpedo boats, as well as a marine battalion reinforced by five PT-76 amphibious tanks: some of these forces eventually reached East Pakistan (since 1971: Bangladesh). However, the most effective way of supporting Pakistan proved the deployment of two Indonesian *Whiskeys* to the theatre of operations. These were submarines RI *Nagarangsang*, (CO Captain Basoeki), and RI *Bramasta* (CO Captain Jasin Sudirdjo). They set sail from Surabaya and marched all the way to Karachi. The liaison officers from the Pakistan Navy were Major Yastur Malik (aboard *Nagarangsang*), and Senior Captain Sultan Ahmed (RI *Bramasta)*: ironically, years later, the two became commanders of the Pakistan and the Bangladesh navies, respectively.[13]

Here the author cannot help but make a digression and draw attention to interesting events that could have happened if the Indonesians had participated in the 1965 war. As we may remember, in the next Indo-Pakistani war of 1971, one of the most successful Indian weapon systems were the Soviet Termit (NATO reporting name: *Styx*) anti-ship missiles, which successfully sank Pakistani destroyers and minesweepers, as well as the PT-76 amphibious tanks, which were at the forefront of Indian attacks in the East Pakistan. So, if the Indonesians had taken part in the war, they would have used the same Termits and PT-76 tanks, but against India. Fortunately for the Indian military, the Indonesians did not take part in the conflict.

Returning to the expedition of the Indonesian submarines to Pakistan, we note that preparations for the transition took place in conditions of absolute secrecy. According to the memoirs of Rear Admiral of the Indonesian Navy, Captain R.M. Handogo (who was a major in 1965), he was originally supposed to be the captain of *Bramasta* submarine, but eventually became the Chief of Staff of Task Force X, and the joint group of Indonesian-Pakistani ships was commanded by Lieutenant Colonel Tedi Asikin Natanegara.

Both Indonesian submarines went to Karachi, but the transition was not easy for them. According to the memoirs of Rear Admiral of the Indonesian Navy Soentoro, who was the navigator of the *Nagarangsang* during the 19-day voyage to Karachi, the submarine more than once experienced various breakdowns. The most serious failure was that of the

Indonesian *Whiskeys* in the 1960s. (Satselhiukencana)

The four *Whiskey*-class submarines 'captured' from the Soviets in 1961 were the backbone of the Albanian Navy until the early 1990s. Though somewhat obsolete, the robust and sturdy boats were the first ever Albanian warships to undertake sorties away from the coast. Maintained with Chinese assistance, they were a trump card in confrontations with Italy. Their importance was underlined by the construction of a massive, 650-metre-long tunnel in the Bay of Porto Palermo, capable of withstanding a nuclear attack while protecting the four precious boats. (Artwork by Anderson Subtil)

Overshadowed by their successors in the form of four Project 633 (*Romeo*-class) submarines, the two Bulgarian *Whiskey*-class vessels never attracted much publicity. In fact, they were the first blue-water submarines of the Bulgarian Navy, capable of operating in any part of the Black Sea. Contrary to the *Malyutka*-class coastal boats from the time of the Second World War, they posed a serious threat to the Turkish Navy, and were also a perfect training tool for several generations of Bulgarian submariners. (Artwork by Anderson Subtil)

Egypt was the fourth biggest operator of the *Whiskey*-class (after the USSR, PR China, and Indonesia), and its vessels served during at least three wars with Israel but failed to achieve any tangible results. While this can be partially justified by the obsolescence of their fire-control-systems and torpedoes – which were near-useless against smaller but faster Israeli warships – Egypt's failure to mine approaches to all the principal Israeli ports using AMD-1000 mines remains inexplicable. (Artwork by Anderson Subtil)

The Indonesian Navy was probably the most successful export-operator of the class: skilled and fast-learning, its sailors managed to utilise all the capacities of their 12 boats to the maximum. Evading British and Dutch search operations, landing special forces operators on Dutch-held islands, harassing Royal Navy aircraft carriers, and cruising undetected off the coast of Australia were some of their most important operations, making them a perfect case study for how to acquire and operate similar vessels by small navies. The first artwork shows one of the boats in original configuration: the other following the removal of their deck-mounted artillery. (Artworks by Anderson Subtil)

The service history of the four *Whiskey*-class submarines of the Democratic People's Republic of Korea Navy is next-to-unknown: photographs of them are extremely rare, and usually taken by US, Japanese, or South Korean forces. Nevertheless, there are two distinct details known about these elusive boats. One, they represented the spearhead of the service for 15 years (until supplemented by more than 20 *Romeo*-class boats), and two, they served as the training tool for generations of North Korean sailors. (Artwork by Anderson Subtil)

Poland was somewhat late to acquire four *Whiskey*-class submarines but set a brilliant example for the proper handling and utilisation of conventionally powered attack vessels. Properly maintained, regularly overhauled and upgraded (at least three times more often than in the Soviet Navy), they proved capable of running cruises into the North Atlantic and were likely to inflict serious damage to any enemy. Indeed, their successful repeated penetration of the Soviet Navy's anti-submarine defences during multiple exercises, as well as break-offs from NATO warships, became a matter of well-deserved pride for the Polish Navy. (Artwork by Anderson Subtil)

A diagram depicting primary weapons of the *Whiskey*-class. (Artwork by Anderson Subtil)

compressed air compressor, as a result of which the boat could not dive. After the submarine arrived in Karachi, repairs were made and soon *Nagarangsang* together with *Bramasta* took part in exercises together with Pakistani warships (after the end of the conflict). Two Indonesian missile boats also took part in the exercise. On the Pakistani side, one submarine and two destroyers were participants of the joint manoeuvres. It is interesting that during the exercises, the sonars of Pakistani British-made destroyers could not detect the Indonesian *Whiskeys*, which became the subject of jokes by Indonesian sailors about the 'invisibility' of the Soviet submarines.

The Indonesian ships received an enthusiastic reception, photographs of President Sukarno were in great demand and were sold in large quantities to the residents of Karachi. Task Force X's mission ended in March 1966. Before sailing home, the Indonesian sailors were invited to a reception with the Pakistani President Muhammad Ayub Khan, during which the Pakistani leader admitted that "without Indonesian sailors, Pakistan could cease to exist." Traditional Oriental politeness aside, there is no denying the fact that India could not ignore the 'Indonesian factor' during the peace talks in Tashkent in January 1966.[14]

During the Indo-Pakistani conflict, the internal political situation in Indonesia itself changed greatly. Due to the consequences of the turbulent events of the autumn of 1965, taking advantage of the mutiny of junior officers of 'September 30' movement, General Suharto came to power, easily suppressing the uprising, and carried out bloody repressions against CPI – the Communist Party of Indonesia (the third largest in the world at that time). As a result of the repressions, according to various estimates, from 80,000 to 1 million members and supporters of the CPI died, and 2 million ended up in camps. On 11 March 1966, President Sukarno was forced to issue an order transferring powers to Suharto, who received the right to act on behalf of the president. The USSR did not break off relations with Indonesia and even restructured the debt in amount of $800 million in 1970.[15] But there was no talk of former friendship and preferential supplies of weapons and spare parts. At the same time, the Soviet Union continued a number of small projects, for example, the construction of three dredges laid down earlier or the completion, in December 1966, of a submarine power supply point at the naval base.

On 9 December 1966, in Surabaya, the Soviet Ambassador to Indonesia M.D. Sytenko and the Chief of Staff of the Navy, Commander of the Indonesian Fleet, Admiral Moeljadi, held a ceremony transferring the Project 055 facility, built by Soviet specialists, to the Indonesian Navy. Project 055 included a power plant, distribution point and charging station installations to supply submarines based on distilled water and high-pressure air. This caused a significant improvement in the combat readiness of Indonesian submarines.

The training of Indonesian sailors also continued. On 2 February 1966, the Indonesian Navy, in addition to those previously trained, sent a number of officers, non-commissioned officers and enlisted men to Vladivostok to receive training to the level of instructors and submarine maintenance specialists.

The change of power in Indonesia (General Suharto finally formalised the seizure of power in the country on 27 March 1968, becoming president of the state) greatly weakened the position of the fleet, which had always been considered the stronghold of the previous president Sukarno. The sailors openly criticised the new regime in their weekly 'El Bahar', published by Sukarno's nephew Commodore Puguh. In early 1969, when Suharto had a fairly secure control of the government and the ground forces, he became closely

One of two Indonesian *Whiskeys* leaving Karachi in March 1966. (via Satselhiukencana)

Indonesian project 613 submarine. (Photo via Forum Sejarah & Militer)

Indonesian *Whiskey* submarines. (Photo courtesy of indomiliter.com)

One of the Indonesian *Whiskeys* at sea in 1971. (Photo courtesy Korps Hui Kencana/Facebook)

involved in the Navy and Marine Corps. All Sukarno supporters were removed from office, and many were arrested. In 1969, Admiral Soedomo, who was Suharto's deputy during the conflict in West Irian (Suharto then headed the Mandala Territorial Command), was appointed to the post of Chief of the Naval Staff. 'Purges' in the navy became widespread. According to Soedomo's calculations, 1,500 naval officers were removed from the army. The generals around Suharto joked gloomily: 'If Soedomo does not stop in time, the fleet will only have ships that will have no one to command.' All reshuffles and new appointments were carried out as a part of the structural reorganisation of the Navy, as a result of which the previous 10 naval territories were converted into three.

Simultaneously with the 'cleansing' of the fleet's officers, the number of warships themselves was reduced significantly. By the beginning of the 1970s, all destroyers delivered from the USSR, the cruiser *Irian*, and most of the patrol ships, minesweepers and fast boats supplied by the USSR were scrapped. The reductions also affected the submarine fleet. To be fair, we note that the submarines were not written off 'to zero' like the destroyers, but, nevertheless, by 1975 only three submarines remained in service with the Indonesian Navy. There were several reasons for the radical reduction of the fleet, and they were all, in their own way, objective. First of all, we note that the anti-colonial movement ended in victory, and a possible full-scale war with the Netherlands over West Irian did not take place, since due to pressure from NATO partners, primarily the United States, the Netherlands gave up control over their last colony in Southeast Asia. As a result, the need to spend on such a colossal fleet (by Indonesian standards) immediately disappeared. And Indonesia, which was in a deep economic crisis, simply did not have money for it. The accompanying transcript of Suharto's conversation with US President Ford in 1975 perfectly demonstrates the state of the Indonesian fleet at that time.

The Indonesians repaired and modernised their submarines whenever possible. In mid-1974, three Project 613 submarines underwent repairs. They became the three aforementioned boats that continued service after 1974. Decommissioned submarines were 'cannibalised' and spare parts from them were used to maintain the remaining submarines in combat readiness.

Let us note that, despite a significant reduction in the Indonesian submarine fleet, the remaining submarines continued to serve 'at maximum', demonstrating in every possible way the best qualities of Indonesian sailors. In the individual reviews of the service of each of the 12 Indonesian submarines, the author will talk about the aggressive and sometimes even arrogant actions of *Pasopati* submarine in the 1970s during joint manoeuvres with the fleets of other countries.

Of the remaining three Indonesian submarines, *Nagabanda* was the first to be decommissioned in 1976 (according to other sources in 1980), then *Bramasta* was retired in 1986, and only in 1990 *Pasopati* was withdrawn from the fleet.

A perfect confirmation of the enormous role of Project 613 submarines in the development of the Indonesian Navy, and the overall emotional assessment of submarines of this type in Indonesia, was the installation of *Pasopati* submarine on 27 July 1998 as a museum in the park in Surabaya. Since then, the former Soviet submarine has been one of the main tourist attractions in Surabaya.

Next, we will move on to a more detailed description of the careers of each of the submarines in the Indonesian fleet. Switching to these descriptions, we note that all the names of the submarines were taken from the mythological names of the weapons of the characters of the Wayang folk theatre. In turn, most of the plots of the Wayang theatre are taken from the Indian epics Ramayana and Mahabharata.

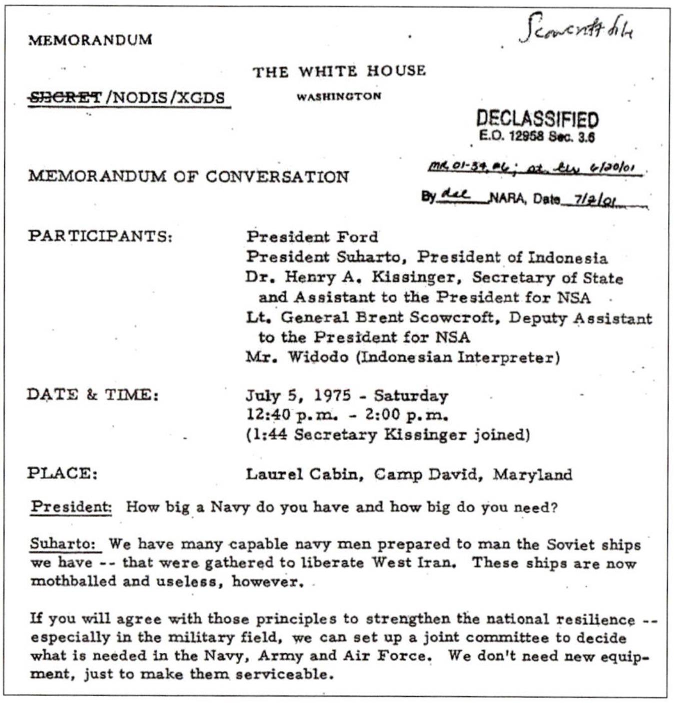

MEMORANDUM

THE WHITE HOUSE

WASHINGTON

~~SECRET~~/NODIS/XGDS

DECLASSIFIED
E.O. 12958 Sec. 3.6

MEMORANDUM OF CONVERSATION

PARTICIPANTS: President Ford
President Suharto, President of Indonesia
Dr. Henry A. Kissinger, Secretary of State and Assistant to the President for NSA
Lt. General Brent Scowcroft, Deputy Assistant to the President for NSA
Mr. Widodo (Indonesian Interpreter)

DATE & TIME: July 5, 1975 - Saturday
12:40 p.m. - 2:00 p.m.
(1:44 Secretary Kissinger joined)

PLACE: Laurel Cabin, Camp David, Maryland

President: How big a Navy do you have and how big do you need?

Suharto: We have many capable navy men prepared to man the Soviet ships we have -- that were gathered to liberate West Iran. These ships are now mothballed and useless, however.

If you will agree with those principles to strengthen the national resilience -- especially in the military field, we can set up a joint committee to decide what is needed in the Navy, Army and Air Force. We don't need new equipment, just to make them serviceable.

Declassified memorandum of a 5 July 1975 meeting between US President Ford and Indonesian President Suharto that describes the decay of Soviet warships in Indonesian service. (Photo via https://m-tsyganov.livejournal.com/307933.html)

A photograph that perfectly demonstrates the gradual decline of Indonesia's submarine force. (Photo courtesy Korps Hui Kencana/Facebook)

Indonesian Naval Academy cadets undergo training on one of the few remaining Project 613 submarines, in 1977. (Photo courtesy Korps Hui Kencana/Facebook)

The famous photograph of the submarine *Widjajadanu*, which gives an idea of the service life of the Indonesian *Whiskeys*. (Photo via Indonesian Internet)

RI *Tjakra*

Submarine *S-91* of Project 613 was laid down on 27 October 1953, at shipyard No.444, named after A. Marty, in the city of Nikolaev. Launched on 23 December 1953, in June 1954 she passed acceptance tests in Sevastopol and entered service on 28 August 1954.

In the autumn of 1954, she moved (within the interior water communications of the USSR) to the north, based in the city of Polyarny, and on 11 November 1954 she became a part of the Soviet Northern Fleet. In July-August 1955, she made a transition to the Far East as part of the EON-65 expedition and on 7 September 1955 she became a part of the Soviet Pacific Fleet, based in Tarya Bay (Krashennikov Bay). From 22 August to 20 September 1956, the submarine made a trip to the Midway Atoll area for reconnaissance. In autumn 1957, she underwent repairs at Dalzavod in Vladivostok, and in the spring of 1959, she went to sea with the officers of the Chinese Navy to demonstrate the capabilities of Project 613 submarines. In August 1959, she sailed from Vladivostok to the port of Surabaya for transfer to the Indonesian Navy. On 12 September 1959, she was transferred to the Indonesian Navy, received the name RI *Tjakra* and pennant number S-01, soon changed to 401. The submarine was named after the Indian mythical weapon, which has a round shape with a pointed outer edge, the earliest records of which are found in the fifth century BC in Indian epics Mahabharata and Ramayana, where *tjakra* is the weapon of the god Vishnu. The first commander of the submarine was Major R.P. Poernomo.

Indonesian Navy submarine *Tjakra* in 1960, in Ambon Bay, Maluku, with original pennant number S-01. (Photo from Indonesian Internet)

Tjakra took part in the Indonesian Navy Day celebrations on 5 December 1960. During the celebrations, the submarine dived into the waters of the Strait of Madura and also landed a group of navy commandos who carried out demonstration underwater explosions and then landed on the shore right in front of the podium where Indonesian President Sukarno was watching and presented him with a festive souvenir. Then the submarine also surfaced in front of the podium with Sukarno, and the commander of the boat, Major Poernomo, who was on the bridge, saluted the president of the country. It is interesting to note that since then, submarines have not dived into

Submarine *Pasopati* as a museum in a park in Surabaya. (Photo via https://www.indomiliter.com/)

the waters of the Madura Strait due to its shallow depth and strong underwater currents.

The appearance of the new submarine at the Indonesian Navy Festival aroused great enthusiasm within the country and received wide coverage in the foreign press.

Tjakra was a part of the Indonesian Navy forces participating in Operation Trikora in 1961-1962, which aimed to capture and annex the Dutch overseas territory of New Guinea. *Tjakra* was decommissioned in 1972.

The future commodore (Indonesian: Laksamana Pertama) of the Indonesian Navy, Raden Pandji Poernomo was born on 18 August 1926, in Surabaya, to an aristocratic family of Indonesian diplomats, and at the time Indonesia gained independence (1945), he was already a member of the Maritime People's Security Agency, which was the forerunner of the Indonesian fleet. He received his naval education in England and France. He was among the first Indonesian sailors to train as submariners at the Polish Navy base in Gdynia (or rather, in its suburb of Oxywie) in the period 1958-1959. He passed all his exams with flying colours and earned the praise of the Soviet admiral for successfully conducting an emergency training dive.

After training in Poland, he arrived by train in Vladivostok and participated in the passage to Surabaya on the submarine *S-91* (in Indonesia she was renamed to *Tjakra*), of which he became the commander after arriving in Indonesia. Simultaneously to his appointment as the commander of submarine *Tjakra*, on the same day, 12 September 1959, he was appointed the commander of the submarine division (Indonesion: DIVKASEL). Then, on 1 November 1959, he was appointed to the post of Head of the Naval Submariner School (Indonesion: SEKASAL). During this period, Raden Panji Poernomo held the rank of Major in the Navy.

Tjakra (formerly *S-91*) in 1960. (Photo via Jalesveva Jayamahe. 1960. Information Department, Indonesian Navy: Jakarta)

Major Poernomo during training in Poland. (Photo via Indonesian Internet)

Indonesian Navy submarine *Tjakra*. (Photo via *Jane's Fighting Ships*)

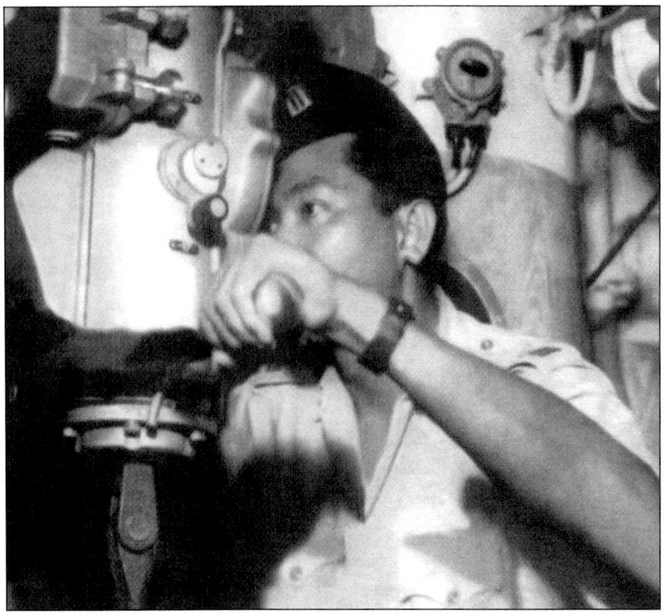

Major Poernomo looks through the periscope of the submarine *Tjakra* during a dive while at the Indonesian Armed Forces Day celebrations on 5 October 1959. (Photo via Indonesian Internet)

Poernomo in 1960, already with the rank of Lieutenant-Colonel. (Photo via Jalesveva Jayamahe. 1960. Information Department, Indonesian Navy: Jakarta)

It was as the head of SEKASAL, in 1961, that Poernomo came up with the motto of Indonesian submariners, which is still used today: 'Steadfast until The End' (Indonesian: 'Wira Ananta Rudira'). In the summer of 1962, at a time of aggravated relations with the Netherlands over West Irian (when the two countries were on the brink of war), Poernomo, already with the rank of Colonel, led a formation of Indonesian submarines (KKS-15) during Operation Trikora. It was he who gave the order for the landing of Indonesian special forces (Indonesian: RPKAD) from three Indonesian submarines in Tanah Merah Bay (the mission was successful only for one submarine). Poernomo also commanded Indonesian submarines during the confrontation around Malaysia in 1963-1964. Subsequently, he went to the USSR and graduated from the Academy of the General Staff in 1968. Commodore Poernomo's career was interrupted in the early 1970s, during the famous purges in the Indonesian navy, when the naval leaders appointed by President Suharto actively got rid of Sukarno's supporters, and especially sailors who could be suspected of leftist views or who were trained in the USSR. Trouble did not escape Commodore Poernomo, who was imprisoned for two years in the Nirbaya military prison, located in the eastern part of Jakarta. Poernomo was saved by his wife, who met with the Chief of the Staff of the Indonesian Navy, Admiral Soedomo, the right hand of President Suharto (the author described his career in his book *Russian and Soviet-built destroyers in service in foreign navies. 1904-2021*). Soedomo reluctantly admitted that 'Poernomo was "clean" but had to be sacrificed because of his sympathies for ex-President Sukarno.'

Poernomo was released, but there was no talk of a further naval career. He was fully rehabilitated (apparently after Suharto lost power in Indonesia) and was buried with full military honours when he died in November 2013.[16] He remained in the memory of Indonesian sailors as the first and very successful commander of the submarine formation, and the slogan of the Indonesian sailors, 'Standfast to the End', introduced by him, is displayed on the submariners' monument in Surabaya (the main part of which is the submarine *Pasopati*).[17]

RI *Nanggala*

Submarine *S-79* of Project 613 was laid down on 18 July 1953, at shipyard No.444, named after A. Marty, in the city of Nikolaev. Launched on 31 December 1953, in January-February 1954 she underwent acceptance tests in Sevastopol and entered service on 30 May 1954. In the summer of 1954, she moved (within the interior water communications of the USSR) to the north, to the city of Polyarny, and became a part of the Soviet Northern Fleet on 2 September 1954. In July-August 1955, she made a transition to the Far East as part of the EON-65 expedition, and on 7 September 1955 she became a part of the Soviet Pacific Fleet, based in Tarya Bay (Krashennikov Bay). In the autumn of 1957, she underwent repairs at Dalzavod in Vladivostok. In the spring of 1959, she hosted a delegation of the Chinese Navy to demonstrate the instruments, mechanisms and weapons of Project 613 submarines. In August 1959, she sailed from Vladivostok to the port of Surabaya for transfer to the Indonesian Navy. On 12 September 1959, the submarine was transferred to the Indonesian Navy, was given the name RI *Nanggala* and pennant number S-02, soon changed to 402. The submarine was named after *nanggala*, a powerful divine short spear wielded by Prabu Baladeva, the Hindu god mentioned in Mahabharata. The first captain of the submarine was Major O.P. Koesno.

Photos like this (President Sukarno participating in a ceremony on board *Tjakra* with Poernomo) did not add sympathy for the disgraced commodore among the new authorities. (Photo via Indonesian Internet)

Indonesian Navy submarine *Nanggala* at sea in 1960, with pennant number S-02. (Photo via Indonesian Internet)

Nanggala (formerly *S-79*) in dock shortly after transfer to the Indonesian Navy. (Photo via Jalesveva Jayamahe. 1960. Information Department, Indonesian Navy: Jakarta)

Nanggala (formerly *S-79*) at sea shortly after transfer to the Indonesian Navy. (Photo via Jalesveva Jayamahe. 1960. Information Department, Indonesian Navy: Jakarta)

Nanggala was a part of the Indonesian Navy forces participating in Operation Trikora in 1961-1962, which aimed to capture and annex the Dutch overseas territory of New Guinea. *Nanggala* was withdrawn from the service in Indonesian Navy in 1972.

RI *Nagabanda*

Submarine *S-218* of Project 613 was laid down on 28 February 1954, at shipyard No.444, named after A. Marty, in the city of Nikolaev. She was launched on 24 May 1954, passed acceptance tests in Sevastopol and entered service on 17 March 1955. In June-July 1955, she moved (within the interior water communications of the USSR) to the city of Polyarny and became a part of the Soviet Northern Fleet on 15 July 1955. From June 1956 to September 1957, during a long transition as part of the EON-66 and EON-67 expeditions, she moved to the Far East and became part of the Soviet Pacific Fleet. She was based in the Far East until the end of December 1961, when, on 31 December, she departed for Indonesia and arrived on 15 January 1962 at the port of Surabaya. On 29 January 1962, transferred to the Indonesian Navy, given the name (presumably) RI *Nagabanda* and pennant number 403. The name of the submarine means 'rope snake' in Sanskrit, used as an attribute in the hands of a giant statue with double weapons that serves as the guardian of a Hindu temple. The first commander of the submarine was Major A.T. Vigno Prajitno.

Submarine *Nagabanda* of the Indonesian Navy. (Photo via Indonesian Internet)

Nagabanda was supposed to be among the Indonesian submarines that took part in the famous Special Forces landing operation at Tanah Mera Bay in the summer of 1962, but an unlucky encounter with a Dutch Lockheed P-2 *Neptune* patrol aircraft off Biak Island disrupted these plans. The boat was on the surface when a Dutch plane appeared from behind. The commander of the boat, Major Vigno Prajitno, gave the order for a sharp dive and soon the submarine was at a depth of 50 metres. The Dutch dropped a sonar buoy and the crew clearly heard the sounds of its operation. The submarine continued diving to a depth of 70 metres. Soon after, the Dutch began dropping depth charges. For three hours, *Nagabanda* swam in zigzags underwater, trying to escape. Depth charges continued to explode around the boat. The situation on the submarine became critical, especially after the submarine's horizontal rudder was damaged. The commander of *Nagabanda* decided to turn off the diesel engine so as not to descend too deep. The boat then began searching for a 'liquid wake': a layer of seawater with a higher density than the surrounding waters. In it, the boat remained completely silent and all noise-producing equipment was turned off. Even the crew was prohibited from moving. The submarine spent 36 hours in this position with the crew sweltering from the heat and lack of oxygen. The submarine then surfaced at midnight to blow out its ballast tanks. From there they sailed to Halmahera Island, where they discovered that the damage to the horizontal rudder had indeed been caused by depth charge explosions.[18] After this, *Nagabanda* sailed to Surabaya and, after quick repairs (the boat was given priority at the ship repair facility), returned to service. It is worth noting that, according to Indonesian data, not only a patrol aircraft took part in the attack, but also a Dutch destroyer, which most likely dropped the depth charges.[19]

The next known stage in the use of the submarine occurred in the period 1963-1964, when, during the period of confrontation with Malaysia, relations with Great Britain and Australia deteriorated. To participate in a potential confrontation with the Australian fleet, *Nagabanda* was sent to the port of Kupang in West Timor. After a day of preparation, the submarine set off on a long voyage towards Western Australia until it was 80km from the Australian city of Perth. It is interesting that at night the submarine moved on the surface, and under water during the day, actively using a snorkel. Finding no activity from the Australian Navy, the boat's commander ordered a return to Kupang. At this point, the team persuaded the commander to throw garbage into the water (primarily tin cans) with the words 'made in Indonesia' in this non-standard way to notify the Australians that Indonesian sailors had visited their waters.[20]

In 1964, at the height of the confrontation with Malaysia, *Nagabanda* was sent to the coast of Trengganu to photograph potential Indonesian landing sites. Two miles off the coast of Trengganu, the boat surfaced and began photographing the shore. As a result, the submarine was discovered by local fishermen who reported her and her pennant number 403. The boat's sonar warned Indonesian sailors about an approaching British frigate and the submarine urgently sailed towards the Riau archipelago and there the crew repainted the pennant number to 410 and sailed back. A British Avro Shackleton-type patrol aircraft discovered a submarine with a new number. The submarine's crew was ready to open fire on the aircraft with a 12.7mm machine gun, but a ban on such actions was received from the fleet headquarters. Thus, the cunning of the boat crew created the illusion among the British that two Indonesian submarines were operating off the coast of Malaysia.[21]

There is some justice in the fact that a submarine with such a bright career in the tense years of the first half of the 1960s was not withdrawn from the fleet in 1974 (like most of her 'classmates'), but underwent repairs in 1974 and continued to serve until 1976 (according to other sources until 1980).

RI *Trisula*

Submarine *S-219* of Project 613 was laid down on 25 March 1954, at shipyard No.444, named after A. Marty, in the city of Nikolaev. She was launched on 10 December 1954, passed acceptance tests in Sevastopol and entered service on 30 April 1955. In June-July 1955, she moved (within the interior water communications of the USSR) to the north, to the city of Polyarny, and became a part of the Soviet Northern Fleet on 15 July 1955. From June 1956 to September 1957, during a long transition as part of the EON-66 and EON-67 expeditions, she moved to the Far East and became a part of the Soviet Pacific Fleet.

Submarine *S-219* on the passage along the Northern Sea Route in the Far East as part of the EON-66 expedition, in 1956. (Photo via https://forums.airbase.ru/)

The first commander of submarine *Trisula* Teddy Asikin Natanegara (to the left), in 1977, already with the rank of rear admiral. (Photo via Indonesian Internet)

Based in the Far East until the end of December 1961, on 31 December she departed for Indonesia and arrived on 15 January 1962 at the port of Surabaya. On 29 January 1962, she was transferred to the Indonesian Navy, received (presumably) name RI *Trisula* and pennant number 404. The name of the submarine denotes the traditional Indian trident, which is a religious symbol in Buddhism and Hinduism. The first commander of the boat was Major Teddy Asikin Natanegara.

The submarine's most famous episode during service was her participation in Operation Dolphin (Indonesian: "Lumba-Lumba"), a special force landing in Tanah Merah Bay on a hidden beach near Kotabaru, West Irian. The details of the participation of Indonesian submarines in this operation have already been described above; we note that the landing of special forces from *Trisula* was cancelled at the very last moment due to active ASW actions from Dutch ships.

Trisula was withdrawn from the service in Indonesian Navy in 1974.

Teddy Asikin Natanegara was trained in the Netherlands, at the Royal Naval College (Dutch: Koninklijk Instituut voor de Marine), in Den Helder in the early 1950s. In 1962, with the rank of Major, he became the first commander of submarine *Trisula* and participated in Operation Trikora. In 1965, with the rank of Lieutenant-Colonel, he led the joint Indonesian-Pakistani squadron as part of the impending participation of the Indonesian fleet in the Indo-Pakistani conflict. From 17 June 1982 to 11 May 1985, he was Deputy Commander of the Indonesian Navy (Indonesian: Wakil Kepala Staf TNI Angkatan Laut).

RI *Nagarangsang*

Submarine *S-223* of Project 613 was laid down on 10 June 1954, at shipyard No.444, named after A. Marty, in the city of Nikolaev. She was launched on 4 August 1954, passed acceptance tests in Sevastopol and entered service on 30 June 1955.

S-223 in Nikolaev in 1955. (Photo via https://forums.airbase.ru/)

In the summer of 1955, she moved (within the interior water communications of the USSR) to the Baltic, and on 20 September 1955 she became a part of the 4th Navy, based in the city of Liepaja. In autumn 1955, she moved from Liepaja around the Scandinavian Peninsula to the city of Polyarny, and joined the Soviet Northern Fleet on 27 February 1956. From June 1956 to September 1957, during a long transition as a part of the EON-66 and EON-67 expeditions, she moved to the Far East and became a part of the Soviet Pacific Fleet. She was based in the Far East until the end of December 1961, then on 31 December she departed for Indonesia and arrived on 15 January 1962 at the port of Surabaya. On 29 January 1962, she was transferred to the Indonesian Navy, and was (presumably) named RI *Nagarangsang* and received pennant number 405. The submarine was named after the mythological snake. The first commander of the submarine was Major Agus Subroto.

In August 1962 *Nagarangsang* took part in Operation Dolphin (Indonesian: "Lumba-Lumba"), a special force landing in Tanah Merah Bay on a hidden beach near Kotabaru, West Irian. The details of the participation of Indonesian submarines in this operation have already been described above; we note that *Nagarangsang* was damaged at early stage of the operation and was unable to land troops.

In April 1963 *Nagarangsang*, as a part of Operation VISHNU MUKTI, together with two other submarines conducted a 'show of force' off the coast of Western Guinea.

In October 1965 *Nagarangsang*, together with another Indonesian submarine, became a part of Task Force X, a group of Indonesian ships sent to support Pakistan during the Indo-Pakistan conflict. On the way to Karachi, *Nagarangsang's* air compressor failed, as a result of which the boat could not dive. After repairs in Karachi, the submarine took part in joint Indonesian-Pakistani manoeuvres.

Nagarangsang was decommissioned in 1974.

RI *Tjandrasa*

Submarine *S-225* of Project 613 was laid down on 29 May 1954, at shipyard No.444, named after A. Marty, in the city of Nikolaev. She was launched on 16 March 1955, passed acceptance tests in Sevastopol and entered service on 16 July 1955.

In the summer of 1955, she moved (within the interior water communications of the USSR) to the Baltic, and on 20 September 1955 she became a part of the 4th Navy. In the autumn-winter of 1955, she moved from Liepaja around the Scandinavian Peninsula to the city of Polyarny, and joined the Soviet Northern Fleet on 27 February 1956. From June 1956 to September 1957, during a long transition as a part of the EON-66 and EON-67 expeditions, she moved to the Far East and became a part of the Pacific Fleet. She was based in the Far East until the end of December 1961, when on 31 December 1961, she departed for Indonesia and arrived on 15 January 1962 at the port of Surabaya. Transferred to the Indonesian Navy on 29 January 1962, she was (presumably) named RI *Tjandrasa* and received pennant number 406. She was named after the ceremonial axe, which has two sharp edges and is also found in Hindu mythology. The first commander of the submarine was Major Mas Mardiono.

In August 1962 *Tjandrasa* took part in Operation Dolphin (Indonesian: "Lumba-Lumba"), a special force landing in Tanah Merah Bay on a hidden beach near Kotabaru, West Irian. The details of the participation of Indonesian submarines in this operation have already been described above; we note that *Tjandrasa* was the only Indonesian submarine that was able to complete the task and land 15 special forces troops ashore. Upon returning to base, all *Tjandrasa* crew members were awarded the highest award, the Sacred Star (Indonesian: Bintang Sakti), by President Sukarno's Decree No.14/1963. This was the only time in the history of the Indonesian Navy that this order was awarded to submarine sailors.

In August-September 1964 *Tjandrasa* participated in Operation KENTJANA, in which the Indonesian Navy deployed four *Whiskey* submarines near the Sunda Strait and Lombok Strait for possible confrontation with the British fleet. *Tjandrasa* was waiting for British ships at the Sunda Strait.

Indonesian Navy *Tjandrasa* submarine. (Photo courtesy Korps Hui Kencana/Facebook)

President Sukarno's visit and speech on submarine *Tjandrasa* on 6 October 1966 became very famous. According to *Kompas Daily*, the submarine was anchored at Tanjung Priok Pier in Jakarta at the time. The speech, which was quite passionate, marked a wave of enthusiasm for the successes of the Indonesian navy. Sukarno concluded his speech with the following words: 'One leap, go forward – there is no way out until victory. Persevere to the end.' (Indonesian: 'Sekali menyelam, maju terus – tiada jalan untuk timbul, sebelum menang. Tabah sampai akhir').[22] 'Persevere until the end' (Indonesian: 'Tabah sampai akhir') has become another of the unofficial slogans of Indonesian submariners.

Tjandrasa was withdrawn from the service in the Indonesian Navy in 1974.

RI *Alugoro*

Submarine *S-292* of Project 613 was laid down on 10 May 1955, at the boathouse of the shipbuilding plant No.112 Krasnoye Sormovo, named after A.A. Zhdanov, in the city of Gorky (nowadays Nizhny Novgorod). She was launched on 29 September 1955. In the autumn of 1955, she was transferred down the Volga and Caspian Sea to the plant's acceptance base in the city of Baku to undergo acceptance

S-225 during tests on the Black Sea in 1955. (Photo from the collection of V.P. Zablotsky)

tests and entered service on 31 March 1956. In the summer of 1956, she was transferred via inland water systems from Baku to the north, and on 25 August 1956 she became a part of the Soviet Northern Fleet. From 25 July 1957 to 14 October 1957, she moved to the Far East as part of the EON-67 expedition and became a part of the Soviet Pacific Fleet on 14 October 1957. From December 1959 to the spring of 1960, she underwent repairs at shipyard No.263, in the city of Sovetskaya Gavan, Khabarovsk Territory. Until the end of May 1962, she was based in the Far East. In May-June 1962 she moved to the port of Surabaya (Indonesia). In July-August 1962, as a part of a separate 50th submarine brigade of the Soviet Navy, she took part in combat patrols in the area of Western New Guinea for potential participation in hostilities on the side of Indonesia in the conflict against the Netherlands. In September-November 1962, Indonesian sailors were trained on the submarine for subsequent acceptance of the boat. On 15 December 1962, she was transferred to the Indonesian Navy, was renamed RI *Alugoro* and received pennant number 407. The name of the boat is taken from another weapon of the Hindu god Prabu Baladeva, given to him by Brahma, in fact it is a very powerful mace with two spikes on each side. The first commander of the boat was Captain S.F. Makalew.

In April 1963 *Alugoro*, as a part of Operation VISHNU MUKTI, together with two other submarines, conducted a 'show of force' off the coast of Western Guinea.

Alugoro gained major publicity as a part of Operation KENTJANA in August-September 1964, the Indonesian Navy deployed four *Whiskey* submarines near the Sunda Strait and Lombok Strait for possible confrontation with the British fleet. *Alugoro* waited for British ships at the Sunda Strait. The British squadron led by the aircraft carrier HMS *Victorious* passed through the Lombok Strait (between the islands of Bali and Lombok) on 12 September, declaring its permanent right to unhindered passage in international waters. The ships prepared to repel attacks by Indonesian warships or the Indonesian Air Force as they passed through the narrow straits. The Indonesians did not dare to start a war. However, submarine *Alugoro*, which detected the aircraft carrier, decided to mark her location to demonstrate the presence of the Indonesian fleet. According to Indonesian data, the submarine was not detected by the British ASW equipment until she surfaced, and her appearance was a shock to the British sailors. After surfacing, she signalled to the aircraft carrier 'Have a nice voyage', receiving in response 'Thank you, the same to you.' This aggressive demonstration of the Indonesian navy's capabilities brought *Alugoro* widespread fame.

The little-known fact of *Alugoro's* participation in testing the Soviet P-5 cruise missile (NATO reporting name: *SS-N-3c Shaddock*) deserves a special mention. The very fact that Indonesia was supplied with such missiles is not particularly surprising, since the USSR did not hesitate to supply Jakarta with the latest weapons. If such a missile was tested by the Indonesians, then most likely it was something similar to a trial modernisation of the Soviet *Whiskey S-146*, with one container for missiles (NATO reporting name: *Whiskey Single Cylinder*). Converting the Indonesian boat into a Project 644 missile submarine (NATO classification: *Whiskey Twin Cylinder*) would require serious modernisation at the Soviet shipyard. The book *Submarine Indonesia* (Indonesian: *Kapal Selam Indonesia*), by Soesilo and Budiman, provides a black and white photograph of the launch of a P-5 cruise missile from *Alugoro*.[23]

However, some details regarding the missile test raise questions. For example, it is said that the tests were carried out in 1962, but we remember that *Alugoro* became a part of the Indonesian Navy in mid-December 1962. In addition, the pennant number of the

A supposed launch of a P-5 cruise missile from *Alugoro* submarine. (Photo via https://militermeter.com)

Alugoro is indicated as 406, while it is usually believed that this is the pennant number of the famous submarine *Tjandrasa*. Be that as it may, it is obvious that the test of the P-5 cruise missile on an Indonesian submarine is another confirmation of the enormous trust on the part of Khrushchev towards his Indonesian allies, as well as Jakarta's readiness to use weapons of psychological warfare (which the launch of the P-5 was) to intimidate the Dutch authorities.

Alugoro was withdrawn from service with the Indonesian Navy in 1974.

RI *Tjundamani*

Submarine *S-391* of Project 613 was laid down on 28 December 1955, at the boathouse of shipyard No.199, named after Leninsky Komsomol, in the city of Komsomolsk-on-Amur. She was launched on 30 June 1956, entered service on 30 November 1956, and on 4 December 1956 she became a part of the Soviet Pacific Fleet. In January – February 1961, the submarine completed a long expedition in the Pacific Ocean. Until June 1962 she was based in the Far East. In July-August 1962, as part of a separate 50th submarine brigade of the Soviet Navy, she took part in combat patrols in the area of Western New Guinea for potential participation in the hostilities on the side of Indonesia in the conflict against the Netherlands. In September-November 1962, Indonesian sailors were trained on the submarine for subsequent acceptance of the boat. On 15 December 1962, she was transferred to the Indonesian Navy, was (presumably) renamed RI *Tjundamani* and received pennant number 408. The first commander of the submarine was Captain R.D. Sudiono.

In April 1963, *Tjundamani*, as a part of Operation VISHNU MUKTI, together with two other submarines, conducted a 'show of force' off the coast of Western Guinea.

In August-September 1964, *Tjundamani* participated in Operation KENTJANA, in which the Indonesian Navy deployed four *Whiskey* submarines near the Sunda Strait and Lombok Strait for possible confrontation with the British fleet. *Tjundamani* waited for British ships at the Lombok Strait.

Tjundamani was decommissioned in 1974.

RI *Widjajadanu*

Submarine *S-239* of *Project 613* was laid down on 29 June 1955, at shipyard No.444, named after A. Marty, in the city of Nikolaev. She was launched on 14 December 1955, passed acceptance tests in Sevastopol and entered service on 24 May 1956. In autumn 1956, she moved (within the interior water communications of the USSR) to Leningrad and became a part of the Soviet Baltic Fleet on 12 November 1956. At the beginning of 1957, she moved to the north, to the city of Polyarny, and became a part of the Soviet Northern

Fleet on 14 February 1957. From 25 July 1957 to 14 October 1957, she moved to the Far East as a part of the EON-67 expedition and becoming a part of the Soviet Pacific Fleet on that 14 October. Until June 1962 she was based in the Far East. In June 1962 she moved to the port of Surabaya (Indonesia). In July-August 1962, as a part of a separate 50th submarine brigade of the Soviet Navy, she took part in combat patrols in the area of Western New Guinea for potential participation in the hostilities on the side of Indonesia in the conflict against the Netherlands. In September-November 1962 Indonesian sailors were trained on the submarine for subsequent acceptance of the boat. On 15 December 1962 she was transferred to the Indonesian Navy, was renamed RI *Widjajadanu* and received pennant number 409. The first commander of the boat was Major Asyr Mochtar.

Widjajadanu was withdrawn from service with the Indonesian Navy in 1974.

RI *Pasopati*

Submarine *S-290* of Project 613 was laid down on 15 April 1955, at the boathouse of the shipbuilding plant No.112 Krasnoe Sormovo, named after A.A. Zhdanov, in the city of Gorky (nowadays Nizhny Novgorod). She was launched on 13 September 1955. In the autumn of 1955, she was transferred down the Volga and Caspian Sea to the plant's acceptance base in the city of Baku to undergo acceptance tests. Entering service on 3 February 1956, in the summer of 1956 she was transferred via inland water systems from Baku to the north, and on 25 August 1956 she became a part of the Soviet Northern Fleet. From 25 July 1957 to 14 October 1957, she moved to the Far East as a part of the EON-67 expedition and became a part of the Soviet Pacific Fleet on 14 October 1957. In January-February 1961, the submarine embarked on a long expedition in the Pacific Ocean. Until June 1962 she was based in the Far East, when in that month she moved to the port of Surabaya (Indonesia). In July-August 1962, as a part of a separate 50th submarine brigade of the Soviet Navy, she took part in combat patrols in the area of Western New Guinea for potential participation in the hostilities on the side of Indonesia in the conflict against the Netherlands. In September-November 1962, Indonesian sailors were trained on the submarine for subsequent acceptance of the boat. On 15 December 1962, she was transferred to the Indonesian Navy, was renamed RI *Pasopati* and received pennant number 410. The submarine received her name in honor of the crescent-shaped arrows that the gods gave to the hero of the ancient Indian epic Mahabharata Arjuna to kill the king of demons. The first commander of the submarine was Captain Sigijoto Sudirdjo.

In August-September 1964, *Pasopati* participated in Operation KENTJANA, in which the Indonesian Navy deployed four Project 613 submarines near the Sunda Strait and Lombok Strait for possible confrontation with the British fleet. *Pasopati* waited for British ships at the Sunda Strait.

However, the most striking moments of the *Pasopati's* service in the Indonesian Navy occurred in the 1970s, when the ship took part in several important manoeuvres and exercises with the navies of other countries.

In 1974, *Pasopati* took part in joint manoeuvres with the Indonesian Navy and the Malaysian Navy to guard the Strait of Malacca. According to Indonesian data, the Malaysian side initially objected to the submarine's participation in the exercises. Perhaps the Malaysians were afraid that the Indonesians on the submarine, under the guise of manoeuvres, would be able to penetrate Malaysian waters. Finally, the submarine's participation in the exercises was agreed, but the commander of *Pasopati*, Captain Soentoro, harboured a grudge and decided to teach the Malaysians a lesson. During the first stage of the exercises, when, after manoeuvres, the ships of the two countries set off for the Malaysian port of Penang, the submarine suddenly surfaced in front of the ships entering the port and seriously angered the hosts. During the second stage, when, after manoeuvres, the ships of the two countries set off for the Indonesian port of Sabang, the submarine again suddenly surfaced at the already moored landing ship of the Malaysian Navy (which was the command ship of the Malaysians in the exercises) and turned on the siren at full blast. Despite the obvious hooliganism, the commander of the Indonesian squadron, Admiral Mardiono (who was himself a former submariner and the famous commander of *Tjandrasa* submarine), only scolded Captain Soentoro with a smile.[24]

Indonesian Navy *Widjajadanu* submarine. (Photo via http://weaponstechnology.blogspot.com/)

Submarine *Pasopati* of the Indonesian Navy and ships of the Malaysian Navy. (Photo via http://weaponstechnology.blogspot.com/)

The next time *Pasopati* distinguished herself was in 1975, during joint anti-submarine exercises of the Indonesian and Australian navies. During the exercise, *Pasopati* acted as an 'enemy' submarine, hunted by anti-submarine frigates of Australia and Indonesia. A fairly modern Australian frigate could not detect the Indonesian submarine and only periodically dropped training depth charges into the water 'blindly'. At some point, the angry commander of the Australian frigate announced that *Pasopati* was not nearby and had gone to port. The Indonesian command gave the submarine the order to surface, which she did, emerging from the water not far from the Australian frigate. Already returning by surface to the base, the Indonesian submariners more than once heard the characteristic signals of the Australian sonar, which continued to track the boat in order to obtain data on her characteristics.

Pasopati on 5 December 1975, during the Fleet Day celebrations in Surabaya. (Photo via *Kompas* newspaper)

Pasopati in the sea. (Photo via http://weaponstechnology.blogspot.com/)

Another photo of the celebration of Fleet Day on 5 December 1975. (Photo via *Kompas* newspaper)

The next time *Pasopati* rose to the occasion was during Operation Seroja from 26 February to 26 March 1976, as a part of the integration of East Timor with Indonesia. The boat was patrolling the coast of East Timor, near the city of Baucau, when the captain of the submarine received information from a sonar operator that the sounds of propellers could be heard, and a vessel was approaching the boat. The submarine rose to periscope depth but did not detect any surface vessel. After additional inspection, the Indonesian sailors were convinced that this was not a surface vessel, but an underwater object approaching the submarine at the speed of 10 knots. Major Soentoro ordered a change of a course, redirecting the boat towards the approaching submarine and preparing the torpedo tubes for firing. However, the fight did not happen, as the unknown 'submarine' turned back and headed home at the speed of 30 knots. Indonesian sailors suggested that it was an American nuclear submarine from the 7th Fleet.

In 1978, *Pasopati*, as a part of an Indonesian squadron, helped to provide security for the ASEAN Summit in Manila, Philippines. In 1979, from 16 May to 20 September, the submarine took part in Operation Halilintar, to combat smugglers exporting raw materials from Indonesia to Singapore and Malaysia.

Pasopati was withdrawn from service with the Indonesian fleet in January 1990, the last of the former Soviet Project 613 submarines. And on 27 July 1998, the submarine was installed as a monument-museum in a park in Surabaya. Since then, the former Soviet submarine has been one of the main tourist attractions in Surabaya.

Inside the museum submarine *Pasopati*. (Photo via http://www.primeportal.net/naval/us_ndaomanu/kri_pasopati/)

Table 1 List of operations and expeditions of submarine Pasopati. (Photo via Universitas Kristen Petra online library)

No.	Nama Operasi	Lokasi	Waktu
1	Operasi Alugoro	Pantai Utara Irian Jaya	28 Juli 1962 – 26 Agustus 1962
2	Operasi Hiu Kencana		01 Oktober 1963 – 02 Februari 1964
3	Operasi Cegat		02 Agustus 1964 – 30 September 1964
4	Latgab Orion	Pasir Putih	24 Maret 1975 – 28 Maret 1975
5	Natuna Jaya	Daeral III	18 Oktober 1975 – 29 November 1975
6	Wibawa VII-1	Timor Timur	17 Februari 1976 – 28 Februari 1976
7	Wibawa VII-2	Timor Timur	28 Februari 1976 – 07 Maret 1976
8	Latgab Philindo Jaya V	Kowihan I	31 Maret 1976 – 09 Mei 1976
9	Natuna Jaya VI malindo Jaya VI	Daeral II	22 September 1976 – 19 November 1976
10	Gladi III/Timur Aman	Laut Jawa	18 Maret 1978 – 24 Maret 1978
11	Timur Jaya V	Indonesia Timur	07 April 1978 – 30 September 1978
12	Cakrawala Baru II	Selatan P. Sapudi	25 September 1978 – 30 September 1978
13	Selindo II	Laut Jawa	20 November 1978 – 24 November 1978
14	Malindo Jaya VII-B	Singkawang	16 Februari 1979 – 03 Maret 1979
15	Natuna Jaya (Obstars)	Daeral I	26 Mei 1979 – 25 Juli 1979
16	Penjemputan KRI Cakra	Laut Jawa	23 Juni 1981 – 24 Juli 1981
17	Operasi Wilbar	Laut Jawa	22 Juli 1981 – 05 Agustus 1981
18	Demo Laut HUT ABRI '81	Cilegon	19 September 1981 – 08 Oktober 1981
19	Mampu Jaya	Laut Jawa	23 Mei 1982 – 29 Mei 1982
20	Kehadiran di Laut	Laut Jawa	22 Juli 1982 – 05 Agustus 1982
21	Demo Laut HUT ABRI '82	Menado	11 September 1982 – 13 Oktober 1982
22	OPS Pam Wilbar	Samudra Hindia	22 Maret 1983 – 13 Oktober 1983
23	Cakrawala Baru IV	Laut Jawa	23 Mei 1983 – 27 Mei 1983
24	Armada Jaya III	Laut Cina Selatan	29 Maret 1983 – 08 Juni 1983
25	Operasi Wilbar	Samudra Hindia	21 Juni 1983 – 30 Juli 1983
26	Operasi Wilbar		05 Maret 1986 – 07 Mei 1986
27	Operasi Jala Mangkara I		11 Juli 1986 – 02 Agustus 1986
28	Operasi Jala Mangkara II		18 Januari 1987 – 06 Februari 1987

Table 2 List of 14 commanders of Pasopati during her service in the Indonesian Navy. (Photo via Universitas Kristen Petra online library)

No.	Nama	Pangal/Korps	NRP	Tahun
1	Sigitjoto Sudirdjo	Kapten Laut (P)	807/P	1962 – 1965
2	Susanto	Major Laut (P)	114/P	1965 – 1968
3	Oentong Sarwono	Kapten Laut (P)	1799/P	1968 – 1972
4	Soentoro	Major Laut (P)	1811/P	1972 – 1977
5	Soeprajitno	Letkol Laut (P)	1814/P	1977 – 1978
6	FX. Murdjijo	Letkol Laut (P)	2647/P	1978 – 1979
7	Hernowo	Major Laut (P)	3151/P	1979 – 1980
8	Bambang Purwadi B S	Major Laut (P)	3988/P	1980 – ...
9	M Jakbar Syafei	Letkol Laut (P)	3939/P	1980 – 1981
10	Bambang Purnomo S	Letkol Laut (P)	5645/P	1981 – 1983
11	Bambang Purwadi B S	Letkol Laut (P)	3988/P	1983 – 1985
12	Sardjun Nurkamal	Letkol Laut (P)	6259/P	1985 – 1986
13	Bambang Purnomo S	Letkol Laut (P)	5645/P	1986 – 1988
14	Imam Zacky NP	Major Laut (P)	7234/P	1988 – 1989

The most famous commander of the submarine *Pasopati* was a naval officer Rear Admiral Soentoro. (Photo via https://kodiklatal.tnial.mil.id)

Indonesian naval officer Soentoro gained publicity for the first time as the navigator of submarine *Nagarangsang*, which in October 1965 sailed as a part of a squadron of Indonesian ships to support Pakistan during the Indo-Pakistani conflict. In 1972, he became the commander of submarine *Pasopati* with the rank of Captain. The period of his command of the boat was the period of the most aggressive and famous expeditions of *Pasopati*. He retired from command of the boat in 1977 with the rank of Major. He later became a Rear Admiral of the Indonesian fleet, and from 1989 to 1990 headed the Indonesian Navy Doctrine Development, Education and Training Command (Indonesian: Komando Pembinaan Doktrin, Pendidikan dan Latihan Angkatan Laut).

RI *Hendradjala*

Submarine *S-235* of Project 613 was laid down on 31 March 1955, at shipyard No.444, named after A. Marty, in the city of Nikolaev. She was launched on 4 June 1955, passed acceptance tests in Sevastopol and entered service on 8 February 1956. In May-June 1956, she moved within the interior water communications of the USSR to the north, to the city of Polyarny, and on 26 August 1956 she became a part of the Soviet Northern Fleet.

From 25 July to 14 October 1957, she moved to the Far East as a part of the EON-67 expedition and became a part of the Soviet Pacific Fleet on 14 October that year. In 1959 she underwent repairs at Dalzavod. Until June 1962 she was based in the Far East. In June 1962 she moved to the port of Surabaya (Indonesia). In July-August 1962, as a part of a separate 50th submarine brigade of the Soviet Navy, she took part in combat patrols in the area of Western New Guinea for potential participation in the hostilities on the side of Indonesia in the conflict against the Netherlands. In September-November 1962, Indonesian sailors were trained on the submarine for subsequent acceptance of the boat. On 15 December 1962, she was transferred to the Indonesian Navy, was (presumably) renamed RI *Hendradjala* and received pennant number 411. The boat is named after Indra's net, symbolic of the power to trap and ensnare your enemies. The first commander of the submarine was Captain R.M. Handogo.

Hendradjala was withdrawn from service with the Indonesian Navy in 1974.

RI *Bramasta*

Submarine *S-236* of Project 613 was laid down on 15 April 1955, at shipyard No.444, named after A. Marty, in the city of Nikolaev. She was launched on 30 September 1955, passed acceptance tests in Sevastopol and entered service on 8 February 1956. In the summer of 1956, she moved within the interior water communications of the USSR to the north, to the city of Polyarny, and on 25 August 1956 she became a part of the Soviet Northern Fleet. From 25 July to 14 October 1957, she moved to the Far East as a part of the EON-67 expedition and became a part of the Soviet Pacific Fleet on 14 October that same year. Until the end of May 1962, she was based in the Far East. In May-June 1962 she moved to the port of Surabaya (Indonesia). In July-August 1962, as a part of a separate 50th submarine brigade of the Soviet Navy, she took part in combat patrols in the area of Western New Guinea for potential participation in the hostilities on the side of Indonesia in the conflict against the Netherlands. In September-November 1962, Indonesian sailors were trained on the submarine for subsequent acceptance of the boat. On 15 December 1962, she was transferred to the Indonesian Navy, was renamed RI *Bramasta* and received pennant number 412. The boat is named after the most powerful weapon from ancient Indian mythology. The first commander of the boat was Captain Leo Darsa.

In October 1965, *Bramasta*, together with another Indonesian submarine *Nagarangsang*, became a part of Task Force X, a group of Indonesian ships sent to support Pakistan during the Indo-Pakistan conflict. Upon arrival in Karachi, the submarine took part in joint Indonesian-Pakistani manoeuvres.

Bramasta was withdrawn from service with the Indonesian Navy in 1981 (according to other sources – in 1985).

Concluding the story about the service of *Whiskey*-class submarines in the Indonesian Navy, we note that the presence of 12 submarines (as well as a number of other types of Soviet ships) in the Indonesian fleet made Jakarta the strongest maritime power in Southeast and South Asia, as well as in Australasia. By contrast, the Australian fleet only reached the number of 6 submarines in its navy by 1976. It is very important to note that the leadership of Indonesia and its fleet very actively used former Soviet submarines for both military and political purposes. Expeditions into Dutch- and British-controlled waters, the demonstrative sending of submarines into the coastal waters of Australia, an expedition to help Pakistan and other similar actions obviously raised concerns among unfriendly states and forces, contributing to the strengthening of Indonesian influence in the region. Another important element to understand when assessing the service of Indonesian *Whiskeys* in Indonesia is their adequate combat capability. There is an obvious cliché that the Project 613 boats, based on German Second World War designs, were noisy and would have little chance against NATO anti-submarine forces. However, actions against the Dutch fleet, and the 'invisibility' of submarines during manoeuvres with Pakistani and Australian ASW forces, indicate that Soviet submarines could quite successfully prove themselves in combat (and this despite the fact that the boats were supplied in simplified export versions).

To understand the atmosphere on submarines while serving in the Indonesian Navy, it is interesting to turn to the memoirs of the Indonesian journalist Sunario Sunarsal, whom the publishing house Berita Yudha sent on 'business trips' three times with Indonesian submarines going to sea (by agreement with the Indonesian military to advertise the fleet's newest submarines). These were *Nanggala* in December 1961, *Tjundamani* in August 1963 and *Bramastra* in June 1966.

S-235 at sea in 1956. (Photo via collection of V. Kazakov)

According to the journalist's recollections, despite the modern equipment, the boats were not designed for sailing in the tropical waters. As a result, instead of air conditioning, the boats had heaters. Accordingly, fans installed on boats were a salvation for sailors from the heat. According to Sunario, 'sweat continues to flow profusely like wrung laundry.' There were no showers on the boats, and the sailors had to be prepared not to wash for a month. Fresh water was used only for drinking and cooking. The real holiday was the raising of the submarines to the surface, when you could swim in the sea. Also, smoking was only allowed on the surface. The toilet on the boats was right under the bridge. Due to the constant use of salt water for various needs, the sailors jokingly called themselves 'salt fish'. They slept on the submarines in any convenient place, with the exception of the commanders who had small cabins. The journalist notes that the sailors servicing torpedo tubes often slept in an embrace with the torpedoes. The most desirable time of the day for sailors was meal-time. At first, the sailors ate perishable foods (vegetables, fruits and meat), and then switched to dry rations. However, as the journalist notes, he has never heard any complaints from submariners. The service was held in full accordance with their motto 'persevere until the end'.[25]

As the submarines aged, many funny stories are told about them. When one of the submarines went to sea in the 1970s, one of her diesel parts failed and, as a result, the boat became much noisier. Relations with the USSR had already deteriorated so much at that time that it was impossible to obtain a spare part. The boat was located near the port of Tegal. The port commander advised the boat commander to contact the blacksmiths in the Pagongan area, who were famous throughout Indonesia. The boat commander acted as recommended and contacted the best blacksmith shop in Pagongan. At first, it was not possible to make a high-quality replacement part, since the sailors, due to secrecy, showed only a drawing of the part and a general diagram of the diesel engine. The replaced spare part made the diesel engine even noisier. When the captain of the submarine made a claim to the blacksmith, the latter demanded to bring not the drawings, but the part that needed to be replaced itself. Having seen the part 'live', the blacksmith laughed and said, 'even

Indonesian *Whiskeys* in the 1960s. (Photo courtesy Korps Hui Kencana/ Facebook)

his apprentice will make one like this.' And indeed, the newly manufactured part replaced the damaged one perfectly and the submarine's diesel engine started working normally again. One of the sailors shouted, 'This is incredible, Soviet goods can be made in Pagongan.'

Soviet submarines received very high praise in Indonesia and to this day they are legendary ships for the population and military of the country. The best evidence of this is the installation of *Pasopati* submarine as a museum specimen in Surabaya.

Indonesian Project 613 submarines in the 1960s. (Photo courtesy Korps Hui Kencana/Facebook)

View of one of the Indonesian *Whiskeys* from cruiser *Irian*. (Photo via Indonesian Internet)

5

OBSCURE NORTH KOREAN WHISKEY

The Democratic People's Republic of Korea (DPRK), if compared to other Soviet allies, began to develop a submarine fleet quite late – in the 1960s. The first submarines put into service with the national navy were four submarines of Project 613. Two boats – the former Soviet *S-75* and *S-90* – were transferred in 1963, and two more – *S-325* and *S-326* in 1966. North Korean sailors were trained on submarines after the submarines arrived in the DPRK. Very little is known about the service of these four boats. We can confidently say that before receiving the first four Chinese-made Project 633 submarines, in the period 1973-1974, *Whiskeys* formed the basis of the submarine forces of the DPRK fleet. As the North Korean Navy became saturated with Project 633 submarines (NATO reporting name: *Romeo*-class),[1] Project 613 submarines began to be used more for training purposes. A number of Russian sources and *Jane's Fighting Ships* wrote about this. Some publications have gone further and claimed that already by 1974 the boats had been scrapped. This is, of course, incorrect, given the tendency of the DPRK armed forces to keep, at least in reserve, very outdated military equipment. In addition, there are references, for example from the famous researcher of the history of the Soviet fleet, Alexander Rozin, that North Korean *Whiskeys* took part in joint manoeuvres with the Soviet Pacific Fleet in October 1987.[2] As for the basing of submarines, we can affirmatively say that in the last years of service the boats were based in the ports of the Eastern Fleet. But this does not exclude the possibility that for some time, especially in the first years of service, the boats could have been based in the Western Fleet (the author encountered such statements).

North Korean Project 613 submarine at sea. (Photo via Stijn Mitzer collection)

The final fate of North Korean submarines raises no fewer questions than the history of their service in the national Navy. According to the website www.militaryrussia.ru, one of the Project 613 submarines, in the summer of 2014, was rusting away in a submerged state with dismantled units to the extreme northeast of Mayang-Do Island. The island is known to be one of the two main bases of the submarine forces of the DPRK Eastern Fleet.

However, as of January 2023, the author no longer found this submarine in the specified geolocation on Google Maps.

On the well-known website dedicated to submarines www.deepstorm.ru, there is a picture of four sunken submarines (in a bay in the central part of the same Mayang-Do Island), which may be of Project 613 submarines.

As of January 2023, the situation has not changed, with the difference that the boats have sunk even further to the bottom, for example, the wheelhouse of the submarine on the far left was already completely submerged.

Here is a brief service history of each of the Soviet submarines delivered to the North Korean Navy.

Submarine *S-75* of Project 613 was laid down on 31 January 1953 in Nikolaev, at the Black Sea shipyard No.444, named after A. Marti. She was launched on 8 August 1953, entered service on 14 December 1953, was included in the Soviet Black Sea Fleet on 23 December 1953 and was based in Sevastopol.

In May 1961, the submarine made the transition through the internal water communications of USSR to the Ekaterininskaya harbor of Polyarny city, however, on 25 June 1961, she went to the Far East along the Northern Sea Route, arriving in Vladivostok in September 1961. The submarine was temporarily assigned to

Submarine *S-75* during sea trials in the Black Sea, 1953. View of the stern gun SM-24-ZIF. (Photo via www.forums.airbase.ru)

S-75 during the passage along the Northern Sea Route to the Pacific Fleet. (Photo via the collection of O.N. Olkhovatsky)

the Soviet Pacific Fleet, and in October 1961 she was repaired in Vladivostok for further transfer to the DPRK Navy.

In the fall of 1962, the boat made the transition to the DPRK, where, after training of the North Korean crew, she was transferred to the DPRK fleet.

Submarine *S-90* of Project 613 was laid down on 12 November 1953 in Nikolaev, at the Black Sea shipyard No.444, named after A. Marti. She was launched on 31 November 1953, entered service on 22 September 1954. She was included in the Soviet Black Sea Fleet on 23 December 1953 and was based in Sevastopol. In April 1961, the submarine made the transition through the internal water communications of the USSR to the Ekaterininskaya harbor of Polyarny city, however, on 5 June 1961, she went to the Far East along the Northern Sea Route, arriving in Vladivostok on 7 October 1961. The submarine was temporarily assigned to the Soviet Pacific Fleet and underwent repairs in Vladivostok for further transfer to the North Korean Navy. In the autumn of 1962, the boat made the transition to the DPRK under the command of Captain 2nd rank B.S. Sukhachev, where, after training of the North Korean crew, she was transferred to the DPRK fleet.

Submarine *S-325* of Project 613 was laid down on 23 July 1955 at the boathouse of the shipbuilding plant No.112 Krasnoe Sormovo, named after A.A. Zhdanov, in the city of Gorky (nowadays Nizhniy Novgorod). She was launched on 29 November 1955. In the spring of 1956, she was transferred down the Volga and Caspian Sea to the plant's acceptance base in the city of Baku to undergo acceptance tests. Entering service on 17 August 1956, in the autumn of that year she was transferred via inland water systems from Baku to the city of Molotovsk (nowadays Severodvinsk). On 19 November 1956, she was enlisted in the Northern Fleet, based in Saida Bay. From November to December 1956, her 2M-8 artillery machine gun was dismantled and the design of the conning tower fence was changed at shipyard No.35, in the village of Rosta. In the period August–September 1962, she went along the Northern Sea Route from the Ekaterininskaya harbor of Polyarny city to the Far East. On 20 October 1962, she was assigned to the Soviet Pacific Fleet, based in Vladimir Bay. In 1966 she was transferred to the DPRK Navy.

Submarine *S-326* of Project 613 was laid down on 31 July 1955 at the shipyard No.112 Krasnoe Sormovo, named after A.A. Zhdanov, in the city of Gorky (nowadays Nizhniy Novgorod). She was launched on 24 December 1955. In the spring of 1956, she was transferred down the Volga and Caspian Sea to the plant's acceptance base in the city of Baku to undergo acceptance tests. She entered service on 19 August 1956. In Autumn 1956, she was transferred via inland water systems from Baku to the city of Molotovsk (nowadays Severodvinsk). On 10 October 1956 she was assigned to the Northern Fleet, based in Catherine Harbour. During the period August-September 1962, under the command of Captain 3rd rank Moskvitin Yu.D., she made the transition along the Northern Sea Route from the Ekaterininskaya harbor of Polyarny city to the Far East. On 2 October 1962 she was assigned to the Pacific Fleet, based in Vladimir Bay. In 1966 she was transferred to the DPRK Navy.

Concluding the rather scant story about the service of Project 613 submarines in the DPRK Navy, only one fact can be stated unambiguously: submarines of this class were the pioneers of the North Korean submarine fleet. They allowed the sailors of the DPRK Navy to gain the necessary experience obviously useful for the future induction of the more than 20 Project 633 submarines, which became a principal part of the country's navy in the 1970s and1980s.

6

FLOATING CHARGING STATION FOR THE CUBAN FOXTROTS

Perhaps the most exotic recipient of Project 613 submarines was Cuba, which received one submarine of this project in 1979. However, the Cuban Navy received not an attack submarine, but a floating charging station converted from one of the *Whiskey* submarines. It is interesting that the converted submarine had already served in foreign navies, namely, in the Egyptian fleet. We are talking about the former submarine *S-175*, which served in the Egyptian Navy on lease as *S-1* until 1967. After nine years of service in the Egyptian Navy, she was returned to the Soviet Union and became a part of the Soviet Baltic Fleet as *S-42*. On 25 May 1970, she was withdrawn from the service as an attack submarine and was converted into a floating charging station *PZS-41* based in Liepaja. In 1977, she was reclassified into a Roadstead floating charging station – *RPZS-411*.

A few words about what floating charging stations are. The task of such stations is to provide diesel submarines with the necessary charging current for their batteries. Diesel-electric submarines need batteries for covert movement under water, when starting diesel engines to power the propulsion electric motors are undesirable or completely impossible. The use of floating charging stations made it possible to significantly extend the life of diesel generators installed on submarines.

The question arises: why did Cuba need such a station? The answer is quite simple – to ensure the charging of the batteries of three Cuban submarines of Project I641K (NATO reporting name: *Foxtrot*-class). These Cuban submarines (the last Project 641 ships built) were delivered between 1979 and 1984. It was for their maintenance, as well as for use as a training vessel, that *RPZS-411* was transferred. The author believes that the floating charging station was also used by Soviet diesel submarines that regularly visited Cuba for joint manoeuvres. These were Project 641B (NATO reporting name: *Tango*-class) boats. Formally, the ship was handed over to the Cubans on 15 March 1979 and arrived in Cuba in the same spring of 1979. However, it was the Soviet crew who kept the boat in working order until the spring of 1982. Obviously, the charging station was actively used until the end of the 80s, when, due to the end of the Cold War and the financial difficulties of the Cuban economy (caused by the cessation of Soviet aid), the Cuban Foxtrots stopped going to sea and were decommissioned, despite their young age, in the 1990s. The former *S-175* was written off and scrapped along with them.

Soviet sailors' photo against the background of *PZS-41* charging station. Liepāja, mid-70s. (Photo via www.deepstorm.ru)

7

CHINESE WHISKEYS

The largest foreign operator of Project 613 submarines was the People's Republic of China (PRC), whose navy had 21 submarines of this class by the mid-1960s. The difference from the fleets of other countries was that these submarines were not imported from the USSR, but were produced in China, albeit using Soviet materials. The production of these submarines in China was a major event for the Chinese Navy and Chinese shipbuilding industry, as it allowed the Chinese fleet to receive a large series of relatively modern submarines and Chinese shipyards, for the first time in history, mastered the production of submarines.

However, the *Whiskeys* were not the first submarines received by China from the USSR. In August 1950, at a conference on naval construction, the Chinese put forward the slogan: 'Learn from the Soviet Navy'. On the one hand, Soviet specialists were invited to train in China, on the other hand, Chinese army personnel were sent to Soviet naval schools and academies to study, and another party (275 people) was sent to Port Arthur (Chinese name Lushun) for training on the Soviet submarines. As a result, in the early 1950s, the PRC received (according to various sources) from 8 to 14 Soviet pre-war design submarines of the *Shchuka*, *Stalinets* and *Malyutka* types. All of these were in the Chinese fleet until the early 1960s, had limited combat capability and served mainly as training ships.

Chinese submarine of the *Stalinets*-class at sea. Above her is a Beriev Be-6 (NATO reporting name: *Madge*) flying boat. (Photo via www.bilibili.com)

In order to obtain more modern naval weapons for the Chinese Navy and master the production of warships in China, the leadership of China and the Chinese Navy held regular negotiations with their Soviet counterparts on the further expansion of naval cooperation. In mid-April 1952, the commander of the Chinese Navy, Comrade Xiao Jinguang, and his deputy, Comrade Luo Shunchu, led a Chinese government delegation to visit the Soviet Union to discuss the 'Naval Agreement'. At the beginning of 1953, Comrade Luo Shunchu went again to the Soviet Union for negotiations. After several rounds of negotiations, the 'Agreement on the Supply of Naval Equipment and Technical Assistance to China in the Construction of Warships' (also known in China as 'Agreement 6.4') was signed on 4 June 1953 in Moscow. The agreement included, in addition to the transfer of four Project 7 destroyers (future *Anshan*-class) and two *Stalinets*-class submarines, the supply of disassembled kits (for further assembly in China) of three Project 613 submarines, four Project 50 (NATO reporting name: *Riga*-class) patrol ships, twenty-four Project 183 (NATO reporting name: *Bolshevik*-class) torpedo boats, four small anti-submarine ships of Project 122bis (NATO reporting name: *Kronshtadt*–class), four minesweepers of Project 254-K (NATO reporting name: *T-43*-class) and ten river minesweepers of Project 151, as well as the transfer of production technologies for these 6 types of warships.

As a result of the signed Agreement, Comrade Huang Jing, the Minister of the First Department of Mechanical Engineering, in July 1954 agreed the Jiangnan shipyard in Shanghai as the head enterprise for the licensed construction of Project 613 submarines. Three ready-made sets of this class of submarines were the first to be assembled, supplied from the Soviet Union. Comrade Zheng Zheng, director of the Jiangnan Shipyard, Comrade Huang Tao, party secretary, and Comrade Wang Rongxuan, chief engineer, immediately took comprehensive measures to build the submarines. Comrade Xue Jianguo was appointed the construction manager and the head of the project supervision team. Comrades Zhou Mingfu, Wu Quanfu, Shen Xiaoliang and Xu Kunyuan were appointed as his deputies. 25 Chinese specialists were sent to study in the USSR.[1]

In 1954, by decision of the Soviet Government, working drawings and technical documentation of Project 613 submarines were transferred to the People's Republic of China for the construction of boats in China. Under the terms of the agreement with the PRC, the first three boats were to be manufactured entirely in the Soviet Union, and then transported disassembled to the PRC, where they were assembled and tested, as was previously done when building boats in the Far East of the USSR. Subsequent ships were to be built in the PRC, with the Soviet Union supplying them with steel for the hull, mechanisms, electrical equipment, instruments and weapons. To provide technical assistance in the construction and development of these submarines, a group of Soviet specialists was sent to the PRC from Central Design Office-18 (Russian: Центральное Конструкторское Бюро-18 or, more often used abbreviation, ЦКБ-18), Central Design Office – 112 and the Krasnoye Sormovo plant, which included A.P. Soloviev, N.M. Vavilov, A.D. Nikitin, K.N. Gordeev and others (about 20 people in total). According to Chinese data, in March 1955, 36 Soviet specialists arrived in the PRC. In the PRC, Chinese specialists with the participation of Soviet engineers translated all design and technological documentation from Russian into Chinese. At the same time, Chinese specialists were trained in submarine theory and familiarised with the features of Project 613 boats, the technology of their construction and testing. At the end of 1957, after the launch of the first three submarines (which were built under the direct control of their Soviet comrades), some of the Soviet engineers returned to the Soviet Union.[2]

Construction of the first submarine of Type 6603 (the name Project 613 received in China) began on 14 April 1955 in Jiangnan, the boat was launched on 26 March 1956, and on 19 October 1957 she became a part of the Chinese Navy (PLAN). The boat became combat-ready in 1958. The boat's pennant number was 115.

The first Chinese-built Type 6603 boat was perhaps the most famous submarine of this design in the PLAN. Exactly 13 years after the visit of Comrade Mao Zedong at the Jiangnan Shipyard,

Construction of the first Chinese *Whiskey* at the Shanghai Jiangnan Shipyard. (Photo via Chinese Internet)

Another photo of Comrade Mao Zedong inspecting the construction of the first Chinese *Whiskey*. (Photo via Chinese Internet)

Comrade Mao Zedong inspects the construction of the first Chinese submarine of Type 6603, 10 January 1956. (Photo via Chinese Internet)

The first Chinese submarine Type 6603, already with pennant number 56-110. (Photo via Chinese Internet)

Right: The first Chinese submarine *Whiskey* with pennant number 56-110. (Photo via Chinese Internet)

Left: The chief engineer of the Wuchang Shipyard in the city of Wuhan, Comrade Sa Benxin (Chinese: 厂总工程师萨本炘), who played an important role in launching the production of Type 6603 submarines. (Photo via Chinese Internet)

the submarine received a new prestigious pennant number 56-110 during a ceremony at the military port of Qingdao. This number indicated the date of the visit of the Chinese leader to inspect the construction of the first submarine of this type.

Subsequently, this submarine more than once became the object of various ceremonial events.

The Chinese submarine Type 6603 with pennant number 56-110 was decommissioned on 14 November 1983.[3]

Note that the first three submarines were built at the Jiangnan plant, and their tests were carried out in Port Arthur.

Construction of submarines in Wuhan began not much later. The first boat at the Wuchang shipyard was laid down in 1956, launched in July 1958 and entered service in December 1958.

A total of 21 Type 6603 (also often designated as Type 03) submarines were commissioned in China. Of these, 13 submarines were built at the Jiangnan shipyard (construction continued until 1964), the remaining eight were built in Wuhan (construction continued until 1962). Five submarines of the project were initially commissioned with artillery weapons in the form of a twin 2M-8 automatic anti-aircraft gun of 25mm calibre (modification *Whiskey-IV* according to the NATO classification), and 16 without anti-aircraft artillery (modification *Whiskey-V* according to the NATO classification).[4]

It is worth noting that there is still no accurate data on the actual number of Type 6603 submarines built. A number of Western and Russian sources believe that the USSR transferred from three to five finished Project 613 submarines to the PRC and, in addition to them, the mentioned 21 submarines were assembled in the PRC. The author did not find information about 'additional' submarines in Chinese sources and believes that the data about them was generated by information that several Soviet submarines were delivered disassembled, but in complete sets, and, as a result, they were mistakenly considered different from those assembled in China's twenty-one submarines.

There is also confusion with the pennant numbers of submarines. So, according to Conway's, the submarine numbers were 119-123, 127, 129, 131, 201-207, 221, 241, 243, 244 and 265-267. At the same time, we remember that according to Chinese data, the first submarine assembled in China received pennant number 115.

There are also unconfirmed reports of incidents with submarines. One submarine allegedly sank on 1 December 1959, after colliding with a Chinese surface vessel.[5] According to Chinese sources, on 2 November 1969, one of the submarines of Type 6603 sank while undergoing repairs at the shipyard and 7 crew members went to the bottom along with the boat. Fortunately, after 10 hours of rescue work, all the sailors were rescued from the boat and the submarine herself was raised to the surface.[6]

Chinese sources provide much interesting information regarding the initial equipment and weapons of submarines of this type. For example, initially only Mars-24k noise direction-finding stations were installed on boats, while Tamir-5L sonars (by that time already installed on Soviet Project 613 submarines) were not supplied to Chinese boats. Only after the launch of production in China of Type 033 submarines – a clone of the Soviet Project 633 (NATO reporting name: *Romeo*-class) equipped with the Tamir-5L sonar system, submarines of Type 6603 began to be equipped with this type of sonar.[7] Submarines of Type 6603 received from the USSR only non-homing steam-gas torpedoes 53-51, which were launched into production in 1951. The SAET-50 (intended to destroy surface ships) and SET-53 (intended to destroy submarines) homing torpedoes were not delivered. As a result, for quite a long time Chinese submarines of this type were armed only with unguided torpedoes. Only after the launch of serial production in China of homing torpedoes Yu-3 (independent Chinese development) and Yu-4 (created on the basis of SAET-50), by the beginning of the 1970s, did Chinese submarines of Type 6603 become armed with guided torpedoes.

Little is known about the service of submarines of this project in the Chinese Navy; even Chinese sources are stingy with information and provide material of a general or speculative nature. Since the induction of Type 6603 submarines into the Chinese fleet, their main task had been to carry out reconnaissance operations in the waters around Taiwan. According to Taiwanese sources, it was submarines of this type that were the subject of the 'hunt' by the anti-submarine forces of the Kuomintang fleet in the 1960s.

As more modern Type 033 submarines began to join the Chinese Navy from the late 1960s, the Chinese *Whiskeys* began to fade into the background. Despite the fact that Type 6603 submarines were re-armed with homing torpedoes and their sonar systems were upgraded to the level of Type 033, they slowly but surely were relegated to secondary roles. One of the main reasons was the increased noise of Type 6603 submarines, while the noise of Type 033 submarines decreased as new modifications for submarines of this type were produced. In the 1980s, the gradual decommissioning of Type 6603 submarines began and, as a result, in the early 1990s the *Whiskeys* ended their service in the Chinese Navy.

It should also be noted that, despite the fact that submarines of this type were landmark ships, both for Chinese shipbuilding and for the Chinese Navy, this type of submarine found itself in the shadow of the next generation of submarines of the Chinese Navy, produced in a much larger series – Type 033, produced on the basis of another Soviet Project 633. However, fully understanding the scale and importance of Type 033 for the Chinese Navy, it is necessary to

Chinese submarine of Type 6603 with pennant number 56-110 at sea. (Photo via Chinese Internet)

remember that it was Type 6603 that formed the basis of the Chinese submarine fleet in the 1960s and would have been at the forefront of the Chinese Navy's attack in the event of a conflict with Taiwan. We should not forget that the expertise gained during the construction, operation and modernisation of Type 6603 submarines allowed the Chinese to maintain the four Project 613 submarines of Albania, the PRC's only ally in Europe in those years, in combat-ready condition. These were the Chinese specialists who carried out repair work on Albanian *Whiskey* submarines in the 1960s and 1970s.

Chinese *Whiskey* with pennant number 266 in port, in 1979. (Photo via G. Keith Jacobs, "China's submarine force")

Chinese submarine of Type 6603 at sea. (Photo via Chinese Internet)

8

POLAND'S BEST WHISKEYS OF THE WARSAW PACT

Of all the operators of Project 613 submarines, Poland was the only country that had extensive experience in the use of submarines even before receiving the *Whiskey* boats from the USSR. Poland entered the Second World War with five submarines (two of them were the latest Dutch-built), and later during the war the Polish Navy received three more submarines from the British Navy. Two Polish submarines were lost during the war (including the newest Dutch-built *Orzeł*), a part of the submarine fleet was interned in September 1939 and did not take part in the war, but the experience and understanding of the strategy of the submarine warfare were well-studied and utilised by the Polish Navy. After the end of the war and Poland's accession to the socialist bloc, the two British submarines that survived the war had to be returned to their former owners. As a result, the Polish Navy was left with four submarines. Three of them, outdated French ones built in the late 1920s, were quickly decommissioned in the early 1950s, and the only relatively modern submarine remained was *Sęp*, a 'classmate' of the lost *Orzeł*. As a result, Poland turned to the USSR to strengthen its submarine fleet. The Soviet Union, which was just starting production of the latest submarines, transferred to Poland six small coastal submarines of *Malyutka* type XV series (Project 96), which in the Polish Navy received the names ORP *Kaszub*, ORP *Mazur*, ORP *Krakowiak*, ORP *Ślązak*, ORP *Kujawiak* and ORP *Kurp*. Despite the fact that these submarines were post-war built, technologically they were a product of the pre-war era of Soviet submarine design and, of course, were of little use as an offensive element in a potential war with NATO. At the same time, these submarines were still quite suitable for the defence of the Polish coast and, most importantly, provided the opportunity to train crews for more modern submarines. Most of the first commanders of Polish Project 613 submarines began their careers as submariners on *Malyutkas*. These obsolete but reliable submarines served in the Polish Navy until the mid-1960s.

The next logical step for the Polish Navy was to receive more modern Soviet submarines of post-war design, primarily Project 613. But for reasons unknown to the author, their receipt by the Polish Navy was delayed. It is funny that it was in Polish Gdynia where the Egyptian Navy got its first *Whiskey* back in 1956, with a 'camouflage' Polish flag, while the Poles only received their first Project 613 submarine at the end of 1962. In total, the Polish Navy received four *Whiskeys* from the USSR between 1962-1965: ORP *Orzeł*, ORP *Sokół*, ORP *Kondor* and ORP *Bielik*. Initially, the submarines were leased, but at the end of 1965, all four boats were purchased by the Poles.

Polish submarines of Project 613. (Photo via Stowarzyszenie Entuzjastów ORP Ślązak i Sympatyków Marynarki Wojennej)

Before moving on to a description of each of the four submarines, a few words about the abbreviation ORP in front of the name of each submarine. ORP is an acronym for the Polish 'Okręt Rzeczypospolitej Polskiej', which translates into English as 'Ship of the Polish Republic'. The author will use this abbreviation only at the beginning of the description of each of the boats, and then omit it thereafter in the text.

Note that from the moment they entered service, the submarines were listed in the 1st Submarine Brigade, and after its disbandment on 18 February 1971 they became a part of the Submarine Division of the 3rd Flotilla of warships of the Polish People's Republic Navy.

On 14 July 1962, a group of 19 officers and non-commissioned officers left for the USSR for training on Project 613 submarines. This group included: Captain-Lieutenant (Polish: Kapitan marynarki) Stanislaw Lorens, Captain-Lieutenant (Polish: Kapitan marynarki) Zdzislaw Glowienka, Lieutenant (Polish: Porucznik marynarki) Jozef Hodurek, Captain-Lieutenant (Polish: Kapitan marynarki) Felix Markowski, Captain 3rd rank (Polish: Komandor podporucznik) Edward Pyzh, Captain 3rd rank (Polish: Komandor podporucznik) Stanislaw Wielebski, Captain-Lieutenant (Polish: Kapitan marynarki) Zdzisław Piórkowski. Here and further Polish ranks are given Soviet analogues.

For three months, Polish submariners underwent training in Kronstadt and Leningrad. There they became familiar with the design, equipment, weapons, main and auxiliary mechanisms and ship systems of Project 613 submarines, and they also underwent training as part of the programme tasks 'Preparing the ship for sailing' and 'Swimming and diving of submarines'. The group returned to Poland on 11 October 1962, ready to receive the first Project 613 submarines.

A detailed service history of each of the Soviet submarines delivered to Poland is recorded below.

ORP *Orzeł*

Submarine *S-265* of Project 613 was laid down on 27 July 1954, at the boathouse of the shipbuilding plant No.112 Krasnoe Sormovo, named after A.A. Zhdanov, in the city of Gorky (nowadays Nizhniy Novgorod). She was launched on 30 November 1954. In the spring of 1955, she was transferred via the internal water communications system to Leningrad to undergo acceptance tests. Commissioned on 30 July 1955 and on 10 August 1955 she became a part of the 4th Navy (from 24 December 1955 – the Red Banner Baltic Fleet) based in the city of Liepaja. In 1960, she took a part in a long expedition to the Atlantic (reached the Bay of Biscay). Before being transferred to Poland, between 15 September 1961 and 15 December 1962, the ship underwent a medium overhaul and was seriously modernised. In particular, the 25mm 2M-8 cannon was removed, the bases for the guns were dismantled, the conning tower hull was rebuilt, the rescue lock was rebuilt, the rapid diving system was improved, four-bladed propellers were replaced with six-bladed ones (the load on the wings was reduced and, therefore, underwater noise was also reduced), a fire protection system VPL-52 was installed. Immediately after factory acceptance tests, *S-265* submarine arrived in Gdynia. On 24 December 1962, at 08.00hrs, accompanied by a Soviet minesweeper and a Polish anti-submarine ship, the Soviet submarine *S-265* with pennant number 181 entered the roadstead of the port of Gdynia. At 08.30hrs the ship moored at the military port of Gdynia-Oksywie. After mooring at berth No.19, eight combat torpedoes were unloaded and the ship's reception began. Sea trials took place on 26 December 1962. The raising of the flag of the Polish Navy took place on 30 December 1962, at 09.00hrs. In accordance with the decree of the Chief of the General Staff of the Polish Armed Forces dated 29 December 1962, the submarine leased from the USSR received name ORP *Orzeł* (English: 'Eagle') and pennant number 292. The submarine received her name in honor of the famous Polish submarine that was lost during the Second World War. In Poland the submarine is often unofficially called *Orzeł (II)*, being the second submarine in the history of the Polish Navy with this name. The flag-raising ceremony was attended by: Chief of the General Staff of the Polish Army Lieutenant General Jerzy Bordziłowski, Commander of the Polish Navy Vice Admiral Zdzisław Studziński and senior officers of the General Staff of the Polish Navy.

To help in training of the Polish sailors, four officers (including the now former commander of the ship, Captain 2nd Rank Anatoly Bernhard) and seven foremen remained from the Soviet crew. Other crew members of the former Soviet *S-265* left the military port of Gdynia-Oksywie at 22.00hrs on 30 December 1962 aboard a Soviet

Soviet submarine *S-265* with pennant number 181, which arrived at the port of Gdynia on 24 December 1962 for transfer to the Polish Navy. (Photo via magazine *Morza, Statki i Okręty*)

minesweeper and headed back to the neighbouring Soviet port of Baltiysk. Interestingly, the remaining Soviet soldiers were at the port on *Orzeł* until April 1963.

The first Polish commander of the submarine was Captain-Lieutenant (Polish: kapitan marynarki) Stanislaw Lorens and the total crew numbered 53 hands.

Immediately after receiving the submarine, the Polish crew began intensive training and study of the ship's systems. The training was based on the knowledge of personnel trained in the USSR and on the technical documentation of the ship. On 19 March 1963, *Orzeł* entered the waters of the Gulf of Gdansk to practice elements of the programme task 'Surface and underwater navigation'. The first dives and snorkelling went smoothly. At the same time, training sessions were conducted by firing practice torpedoes from torpedo tubes. On 2 April 1963, after completing the training of the *Orzeł* crew, the Soviet specialists flew back to the USSR. In the spring and summer of 1963, the ship conducted active training, primarily related to torpedo firing. By the August of the same year, the submarine had entered the North Sea, where she took part in joint exercises with the Soviet fleet, during which *Orzeł* twice detected and attacked a Soviet Project 68-bis (NATO reporting name: *Sverdlov*-class). Successful participation in the exercises served as the basis for the praise awarded the ship by the commander of the Soviet Baltic Fleet. In the period from 14 to 20 September, *Orzeł*, together with another Polish submarine ORP *Sęp* and the destroyer ORP *Błyskawica*, visited the capital of Denmark - Copenhagen. The group was commanded by Captain 1st Rank (Polish: Komandor) Henryk Pietraszkiewicz. The ship moored on 16 September 1963 in Copenhagen, at Langelin Pier. During their four-day stay, the crew visited the city sightseeing including monuments, the weapons museum, ships of the Danish Navy, the Tuborg and Carlsberg breweries, and the royal porcelain factory. The crew also participated in meetings with the local population and Danish sailors.[1]

On the way back, the boat encountered a strong storm. On 17 October, the ship moored at the shipyard named after the Paris Commune in Gdynia, where renovation work took place for 2 months. During the first year of service under the Polish flag, *Orzeł* covered 3,292.3 miles on the surface and 1,366.2 miles under water. Also in 1963, eight training torpedoes were fired from the ship.

In 1964, many changes among the crew took place on *Orzeł*, as a new crew was created for another Project 613 submarine *Sokół* received by Poland. For this purpose, on 8 January, the best six non-commissioned officers and sailors were transferred to the newly arrived submarine. On 17 February 1964, the *Sokół* crew began training on *Orzeł*. In the period from 2 to 18 June 1964, *Orzeł* was on expedition in the North Atlantic. This was the first time a Polish submarine entered the area since the Second World War.

After returning to Poland, the submarine visited Gothenburg and Leningrad, together with other Polish ships, in September 1964 and November 1964, respectively.

On 29 June 1965, the boat, accompanied by another Polish submarine *Sokół*, again set off on an expedition to the North Atlantic. Being in remote waters gave submariners many advantages. This made it possible, first of all, to acquire extensive experience and skills in long-term operation of ship mechanisms and systems in various conditions of surface and underwater navigation. The voyage was a serious test of the crew's psychological endurance and required great fortitude. The Atlantic expedition ended on 27 July 1965. The ship spent 12 days submerged. In 1966, the submarine underwent a medium repair, which lasted from 2 January to 31 October.

The first commander of *Orzeł* submarine Stanislav Laurens. (Photo via Klub Marynarki Wojennej website)

Orzeł on a friendly visit to Copenhagen. (Photo via http://www.kartonwork.pl)

On 11 June 1967, *Orzeł*, along with other Polish submarines, was placed on high alert due to the Arab-Israeli Six-Day War. She was given the task of going out to the Baltic Sea. After returning to the port, the crew began preparing the ship for passage to the Atlantic. This ocean expedition lasted from 20 July to 21 August 1967. In addition to *Orzeł*, three other Polish Project 613 submarines took part: *Sokół*, *Kondor* and *Bielik*. During this journey, the ship covered more than 4,600 nautical miles, of which 814 nautical miles *Orzeł* passed under water.

On 17 May 1968, *Orzeł* together with classmate *Kondor* set off on perhaps their most famous expedition. As a part of this exit into the North-East Atlantic and further passage to the Soviet port of

Colourised photograph of *Orzeł* in 1964. (Photo via The Polish Navy in colour collection)

Orzeł with a temporary pennant number 317, in June 1968. (Photo via "Navy 1945-1970", Wydawnictwo Morskie Gdańsk 1971)

Orzeł as the German *U-94* in the film *Four Tankmen and a Dog*. (Photo via Stowarzyszenie Entuzjastów ORP Ślązak i Sympatyków Marynarki Wojennej)

Orzeł in 1970. (Photo taken from a postcard issued by Biuro Wydawnicze "Ruch". Photographer: S. Pudlik. From the Facta Nautica collection.)

Murmansk, Polish submariners practiced breaking through Soviet anti-submarine defences on the approaches to the Soviet naval bases of the Northern Fleet. Despite the coastal waters being saturated with ASW forces, the Polish submarines were not detected and were able to freely enter the main base of the Soviet Northern Fleet. The submarines returned to Poland on 19 June 1968, covering a distance of 4,873 nautical miles. *Orzeł*, on the way to Murmansk, had a temporary tactical pennant number 317.

In 1968, *Orzeł* acted as the German submarine *U-94* during the filming of the famous movie series *Four Tankmen and a Dog* (Polish: *Czterej pancerni i pies*).

In total, during 1968, *Orzeł* covered 6,450 nautical miles on the surface in 969 hours, and 2,208 nautical miles submerged in 496.5 hours.

In 1969, from 14 August to 11 September, the ship was on an autonomous ocean expedition. The submarine conducted continuous reconnaissance in the area of approaches to the naval bases of Holly Lough (Scotland) and Londonderry (Northern Ireland) and monitored NATO activities in the Baltic Sea, North Sea and North-East Atlantic. During the mentioned campaign, *Orzeł* covered approximately 4,000 nautical miles, of which 500 nautical miles were submerged, for approximately 230 hours. On 1 April 1970, the ship was put into overhaul, which was supposed to last until 29 December 1970.

Eventually, the overhaul was completed on 27 February 1971. On 8 June , the ship participated in the NEPTUNE-71 exercises. Between 2 August and 14 October, the ship was at the Stocznia Marynarki Wojennej (MW) shipyard in Gdynia undergoing dock repairs. Note that most of the repairs of Polish Project 613 submarines took place at this shipyard. In 1971, the ship covered 2,405 nautical miles on the surface in 406 hours, and 796 nautical miles in 229 hours underwater.

In the period from 31 May to 5 June 1972, the ship took part in the exercises of the Warsaw Pact fleets BALTIKA-72. After exercises from 22 June to 27 July, the ship underwent dock repairs at the shipyard in Gdynia.

The tenth anniversary of the raising of the Polish flag was celebrated by *Orzeł* on 13 January 1973. At this point, the ship's service life in the navies of the USSR and Poland was already 17 and a half years, and, due to wear and tear on the ship's hull, the maximum permissible diving depth was reduced from 170 to 120 metres. On 16 May 1973, the ship was docked at the MW shipyard. From 4 September to 13 September 1974, exercises of the naval forces of the Warsaw Pact countries, FALA-74, took place. *Orzeł* was recognised as the best ship in the class of submarines at these exercises. In the period from 1 to 11 October 1974, *Orzeł* took part in a friendly visit to DDR, based from 5 to 9 October in Rostock. On 2 January 1975, the ship was put to the shipyard in Gdynia for a medium overhaul. In July 1975, the boat took part in POSEIDON-75 exercises. Note that despite the gradual ageing of the ship, the intensity of its use did not decrease, so in 1976, *Orzeł* covered 4,296.4 nautical miles on the surface in 564.4 hours, and 1,541.3 nautical miles underwater in 470.8 hours. The ship was anchored for 362 hours and submerged 127 times.

Based on the results of intensive service in 1977 and the successful 15-year operation as part of the Polish fleet, the ship was awarded the title of 'Leading Naval Combat Ship' (Polish: *"Najlepszy okręt Marynarki Wojennej"*).

In 1978, the crew decided to intensify their training furthermore, in order to achieve the best results. The ship took part in LATO-78 exercises, receiving a very good rating. On 12 October, the

Loading a torpedo onto *Orzeł* in the autumn of 1972. (Photo via "Morza, Statki i Okręty" magazine)

The stern of the submarine *Orzeł* (in the foreground), undergoing mid-term repairs at the MW shipyard in Gdynia. March 1976. (Photo via "Morza, Statki i Okręty" magazine)

celebrations on the occasion of the 35th anniversary of the Polish Army ended. The ship's crew participated in all the events accompanying this military holiday. The year 1979 began with a mid-term repair of the ship. Already on 9 January, *Orzeł* was placed at the shipyard in Gdynia. On 10 June, the ship was moored for repairs and maintenance of the underwater hull. The ship left dock on 5 July to continue her mid-overhaul, which was completed on 19 October 1979.

In March 1980, *Orzeł* was sent to the shipyard in Gdynia for repairs to the ballast tanks and their fittings.

On 16 June, the ship's crew welcomed the first Polish pilot-cosmonaut, Mirosław Hermaszewski.

In October 1980, the submarine took part in 14-day exercises together with the anti-submarine forces of the People's Navy of the DDR. There were also East German sailors on board the submarine. On 24 October, the ship dived to a depth of 124m. The hull turned out to be sealed, the mechanisms worked properly.

The year 1981 began with the crew fully prepared to carry out the tasks assigned to them. But the ship's hull was further deteriorated according to test results and the recommendation of the Technical Commission, which reduced her diving depth from 120 to 100m. After the introduction of martial law in Poland on 13 December 1981, an Emergency Response Team was created from part of the submarine's crew, their task was to ensure the security of military facilities. The group consisted of one officer, three non-commissioned officers and seven sailors.

Orzeł in the port of Gdynia-Oksywie in May 1980. (Photo via *Morza, Statki i Okręty* magazine)

The first Polish cosmonaut Miroslaw Giermaszewski looks through the periscope of the submarine *Orzeł*. (Photo via *Morza, Statki i Okręty* magazine)

The crew of *Orzeł* in 1981. (Photo via *Morza, Statki i Okręty* magazine)

In the period from 31 May to 4 June 1982, *Orzeł* was at sea performing tasks as a part of the Combined Warsaw Pact squadron in the Baltic Sea. The ship's actions were highly appreciated by the command. Sadly, 1983 was the last year of service of the ship under the Polish flag. Until the late autumn of 1983, the crew competed for the title of the best submarine of the Polish Navy, but the technical condition of the ship deteriorated and, in accordance with the order of the Commander-in-Chief of the Navy No.0132, as of 30 December 1983, *Orzeł* ended her service in the Polish Navy. During the flag lowering ceremony on the ship, a large delegation of former commanders, officers and sailors of the submarine, as well as many invited guests of honour, were present. After reading the order of the commander of the Polish Navy dated 30 December 1983, in which he indicated the place and role of *Orzeł* in the history of the Polish Navy, the command was given: 'The flag of the Polish People's Navy on the *Orzeł* to be lowered.'

During 21 years of service under the Polish flag, the ship performed many important tactical and special missions. The ship won the title of 'Leading Ship of the Navy' four times – in 1963, 1965, 1972 and 1977. The submarine participated in long Atlantic expeditions six times. In 1974, she was recognised as the best submarine in joint exercises of the allied navies of the Warsaw Pact countries. During her service under the Polish flag, *Orzeł* covered a total of about 90,000 nautical miles, of which about 30,000 were underwater.

In 1986, the submarine's hull was towed to Świnoujście, where it was cut into scrap metal. Some pieces of equipment, a commemorative plaque and the letters of the ship's name were donated to the Naval Museum.

During the service of *Orzeł* submarine in the Polish Navy, she was commanded by the following officers (Polish military ranks are given Soviet equivalents):

- Captain-Lieutenant Stanislaw Lorens (Polish: Kapitan marynarki): 30 December 1962 – 21 September 1964
- Captain-Lieutenant Ryszard Miecznikowski (Polish: Kapitan marynarki): 21 September 1964 – 9 September 1968
- Captain 3rd rank Zdislaw Głowienka (Polish: Komandor podporucznik): 7 November 1968 – 4 November 1969
- Captain-Lieutenant Adam Lang (Polish: Kapitan marynarki): 5 November 1969 – 7 July 1976
- Captain-Lieutenant Henryk Kula (Polish: Kapitan marynarki): 4 August 1976 – 10 December 1979
- Captain 3rd rank Edward Olewiński (Polish: Komandor podporucznik): 10 December 1979 – 8 March 1983
- Captain-Lieutenant Ryszard Latos (Polish: Kapitan marynarki): 8 March 1983 – 30 December 1983

The second commander of *Orzeł* submarine, Ryszard Miecznikowski, was born on 30 January 1933, in the village of Chernilo, Kostopol district, Volyn voivodeship of Poland (territory of present-day Ukraine). On 5 June 1951 he entered the Naval Officers School (Polish: Oficerska Szkoła Marynarki Wojennej). After graduating in 1955, with the rank of Podporucznik marynarki (Soviet equivalent – Lieutenant), he was sent to the 1st Submarine Brigade and appointed the commander of the navigation and communications department on *Krakowiak* submarine (Soviet Project 96 *Malyutka*). In 1957, he was promoted to the rank of Porucznik marynarki (Soviet equivalent – Senior Lieutenant) and the following year became deputy commander of the aforementioned submarine. Subsequently, he was transferred to the position of deputy commander of the submarine

The second commander of *Orzeł* submarine Ryszard Miecznikowski. (Photo: Club Marynarki Wojennej)

Captain-Lieutenant Ryszard Miecznikowski looks through the periscope of the submarine *Orzeł*, 1965. (Photo via *Morza, Statki i Okręty* magazine)

Ślązak (also Project 96 *Malyutka*). In 1961, he was sent to a course for submarine commanders, and after graduating, he became the commander of *Mazur* submarine (again Project 96 *Malyutka*). Two years later, as Kapitan marynarki (Soviet equivalent – Captain-Lieutenant), he was appointed deputy commander of the newly created Project 613 submarine formation, and five months later, on 21 September 1964, he took command of the submarine *Orzeł*.

Ryszard Miecznikowski commanded *Orzeł* until 9 September 1968 and left the boat with the rank of Komandor podporucznik (Soviet equivalent – Captain 3rd rank). In the same 1968, after 13 years of service on submarines, he was sent to study at the Naval Academy of the Order of Lenin in the city of Leningrad. Returning to Poland in 1971, he took up the duties of a senior lecturer at the Department of Naval Command Tactics at the Higher School of Naval Forces (Polish: Wyższa Szkoła Marynarki Wojennej) in Gdynia. In 1972, already with the rank of Komandor porucznik (Soviet equivalent – Captain 2nd rank), he entered full-time doctoral studies at the Naval Academy in Leningrad. After its completion in 1977, he was appointed deputy head of the department of 'Operational Art and Tactics of Naval Services', and, in 1984, to the position of head of this department. He retired in 1991 but continued to take an active part in events related to the activities and functioning of the Polish Navy. He co-authored the book *The Art of Naval Operations* (Polish: Sztuka operacyjna Marynarki Wojennej). Already as a reserve officer, he participated in the development of the concept of naval defence operations. He was awarded many orders and medals, including, among others, the gold medal of the Armed Forces in the service of the Fatherland, the gold Cross of Merit, the Knight's Cross of the Renaissance of Poland. He died suddenly on 30 March 2001 at the age of 68.

ORP *Sokół*

Submarine *S-278* of Project 613 was laid down on 27 July 1954, at the boathouse of the shipbuilding plant No.112 Krasnoe Sormovo, named after A.A. Zhdanov, in the city of Gorky (nowadays Nizhny Novgorod). She was launched on 19 April 1955. In the spring of 1955, she was transferred to the city of Leningrad along the inland water systems of the USSR, where she underwent acceptance tests. Entering service on 12 November 1955, on 26 November 1955 she was enlisted in the 8th Navy (from 24 December 1955 – Red Banner Baltic Fleet). By 1 December 1956 she was withdrawn from the Soviet Baltic Fleet and was mothballed in the harbour of the city of Paldiski (nowadays a part of Estonia), and later was again mothballed in the city of Ust-Dvinsk (nowadays a part of Latvia). Reactivated on 15 July 1964 for further transfer to the Polish Navy.

On 19 October 1964 submarine *S-278* (pennant number 375) entered the port of Oksiwi (a suburb of Gdynia). On 22 October 1964, sea trials began. By order as of 23 October 1964, the Chief of the General Staff included the former *S-278* under the new name ORP *Sokół* (English: 'Falcon') with pennant number 293 into the Polish Navy. The submarine received her name in honour of the famous Polish submarine (British-built type U), which successfully fought during the Second World War in the Mediterranean Sea. The submarine is often unofficially called ORP *Sokół (II)* in Poland, as she was the second submarine in the history of the Polish Navy with this name. On 24 October 1964, the Commander-in-Chief of the Polish Navy ordered the commander of the 1st Submarine Brigade to accept *Sokół* and raise the Polish flag on her. Command of the ship was taken by Captain-Lieutenant (Polish: Kapitan marynarki) Wladislav Janeczek. By the time the boat was handed over to the Polish fleet, the crew had already been prepared, as the future crew of the submarine had been training on the first boat of Project 613 of the Polish Navy *Orzeł* since February 1964.

By 3 December 1964 *Sokół* was at sea to support the return to port of the submarine *Sęp* (pre-war Dutch built) that had suffered an explosion and fire in its battery compartment. From 29 June 1965 to 27 July 1965, the submarine was on a tactical and navigational cruise in the North Sea and the Northeast Atlantic. From 13 August 1965 to 25 September 1965 the submarine underwent repairs at the MW shipyard in Gdynia. On 4 December 1965 *Sokół* made a test dive into the Gotland Basin to a depth of 170m.

From 28 June 1966 to 29 July 1966, the submarine was on an autonomous cruise in the North Sea and North-East Atlantic with two other Polish *Whiskeys* – *Kondor* and *Bielik*. From 12 September 1966 to 20 December 1966, she was under repair at the MW shipyard. From 20 July 1967 to 21 August 1967, the submarine was on an ocean operational training campaign to the North Sea and

Sokół on 27 June 1965 in the Bay of Gdynia, during the celebration of Navy Day. (Photo https://facta-nautica.graptolite.net/)

Sokół during a friendly visit to Stockholm. (Photo via Stowarzyszenie Entuzjastów ORP Ślązak i Sympatyków Marynarki Wojennej)

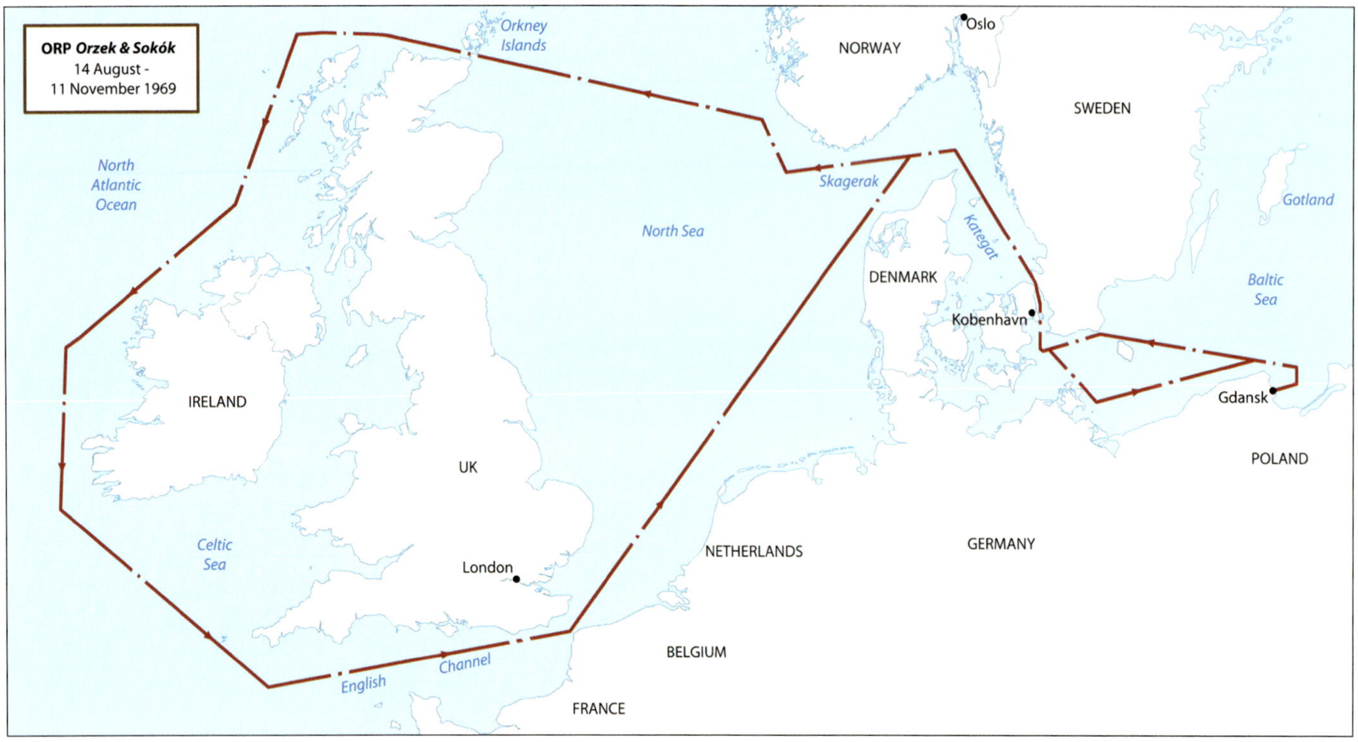

A map showing the route of *Sokół* submarine in the North Sea and North-East Atlantic in 1969. (Map by b.b.h.illustrations, based on Stowarzyszenie Entuzjastów ORP Ślązak i Sympatyków Marynarki Wojennej)

Northeast Atlantic, visiting the port of Murmansk together with three other Polish submarines of Project 613. During the expedition, the boat received a temporary pennant number 313. From 20 to 27 September1967 she was with the submarine *Sęp* on a friendly visit to Stockholm.

On 10 October 1967 *Sokół* was recognised as 'The Leading ship of the Polish Navy'. From 15 October 1967 to 20 May 1968, she underwent repairs at the MW shipyard. On 1 September 1969, the submarine dived 180m deep into the Gotland Basin. From 14 August 1969 to 11 September1969, the submarine carried out a combat training campaign in the North Sea and the Northeast Atlantic.

From 23 to 26 September 1969, the submarine took part in the Warsaw Pact navies' exercises Odra-Nisa-69. On 20 October 1969 *Sokół* was again recognised as the 'Leading ship of the Polish Navy'. From 21 May 1970 to 15 June 1970 the boat underwent repairs at the MW shipyard dock. In June 1970, the ship was temporarily assigned pennant number 296.

From 10 September 1970 to 8 October 1970, the boat, together with another Polish *Whiskey Bielik*, was on a combat training cruise in the North-East Atlantic. From 30 May 1971 to 8 June 1971, the submarine took part in Reda-71 and Neptune-71 exercises, and from 5 to 8 July 1971 participated in Soyuz-71 exercises of the Warsaw Pact countries. From January to September 1972, the boat underwent repairs at the MW shipyard. From 1 March 1973 to 3 April 1973 *Sokół* underwent a warranty inspection at the MW shipyard. On 1 July 1973 the boat went to sea with the First Secretary of the Polish United Workers' Party Edward Gierek, Prime Minister Piotr Jaroszewicz, Secretary of the Provincial Committee in Gdansk Tadeusz Bejm and the Minister of National Defence, Lieutenant General Wojciech Jaruzelski on board. From 17 August 1973 to 27 August 1973, the submarine took part in Neptune-73 exercises. In October 1973, for the third time during her service in the Polish Navy, she received the title of 'Leading Ship of the Fleet'.

Sokół with temporary pennant number 296. (Photo via Stowarzyszenie Entuzjastów ORP Ślązak i Sympatyków Marynarki Wojennej)

From 1 October 1974 to 11 November 1974, the submarine, together with two other Polish *Whiskeys Kondor* and *Bielik*, was on a friendly visit to DDR. On 28 October 1974 *Sokół* was again recognised as the 'Leading Ship of the Navy'. From 27 February 1975 to 26 March 1975 the ship underwent a major overhaul at the MW shipyard. On 18 June 1975, the submarine took part in Poseidon-75 exercises and on 5 August 1975, in Dolphin-75 exercises of the Warsaw Pact countries. From 4 January 1976 to 31 July 1976, the submarine underwent a medium overhaul at the MW shipyard. From 16 to 21 May 1977, *Sokół* took part in Reda-77 exercises, and from 29 to 30 June 1977, in the Warsaw Pact fleets' Fala-77 exercises. From 27 March 1978 to 5 April 1978, the submarine took part in joint exercises with the DDR Navy in the Sassnitz and Arkona areas. From 17 June 1978 to 18 July 1978, the boat underwent repairs at the MW shipyard. From 14 to 19 August 1978, the submarine was on a friendly visit to Karlskrona, Sweden. On 2 October 1978 *Sokół* was recognised as the 'Leading Ship of the Navy' for the fifth time. On 4 October 1978, the submarine dived 120m deep into the Gotland Basin.

From 5 to 28 July 1979 the ship underwent another repair at the MW shipyard. From 2 to 5 October 1979, the boat was on a navigational campaign, during which it dived to a depth of 120m into the Gotland Basin. From 2 January 1980 to 31 July 1980, the submarine underwent a major overhaul at the MW shipyard. From 3 to 5 March 1981, the boat took part in ZOP exercises of the DDR Navy, and from 18 to 21 March 1981 participated in Fala-81 exercises of the Warsaw Pact countries. From 25 April 1981 to 29 May 1981 *Sokół* underwent repairs at the MW shipyard. After the introduction of martial law in Poland on 13 December 1981, a Rapid Response Group was created from a part of the submarine's crew, whose task was to ensure the security of military facilities. The group consisted of one officer, four non-commissioned officers and seven sailors. From 8 to 20 March 1982, the submarine took part in ZOP exercises of the DDR Navy, and from 1 to 11 June 1982 participated in Squadron-82 exercises in the North Sea. From 25 February 1983 to 7 April 1983, the submarine was under repair at the MW shipyard. From 3 to 20 May 1983, *Sokół* took part in Reda-83 exercises, and from 3 to 9 June 1983 participated in Soyuz-83 Warsaw Pact navies' exercises. From January 1984, the ship underwent repairs at the MW shipyard.

From 1 March 1985 to 4 April 1985 the submarine took part in Polygon-85 exercises. From 15 April 1985 to 29 May 1985 the boat underwent another repair at the MW shipyard. On 3 June 1985, *Sokół* took part in the exercises Reda-85 and from 17 to 20 June 1985 participated in Barracuda-85 exercises of the Warsaw Pact countries. In June 1986, the boat took part in Rekin-86 Warsaw Pact fleets' exercises. In 1987, *Sokół* was reclassified into a combat training ship and on 12 December 1987 she was withdrawn from the service with the Polish Navy.[2]

The submarine's hull was towed to the MW shipyard in Gdynia and scrapped in 1989.

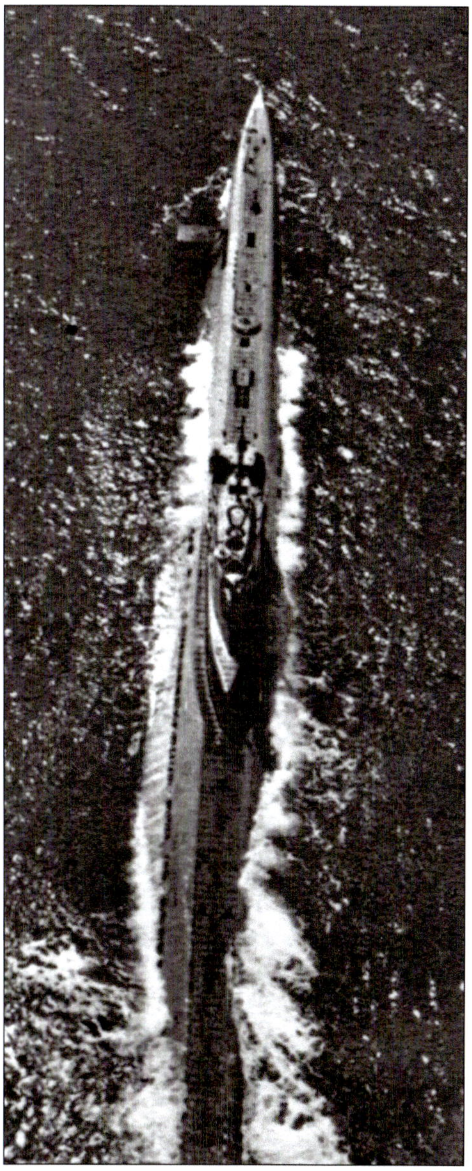

Sokół at sea. (Photo via Stowarzyszenie Entuzjastów ORP Ślązak i Sympatyków Marynarki Wojennej)

Sokół at sea in 1978. (Photo via Stowarzyszenie Entuzjastów ORP Ślązak i Sympatyków Marynarki Wojennej)

Sokół in the early 80s. (Photo via Stowarzyszenie Entuzjastów ORP Ślązak i Sympatyków Marynarki Wojennej)

During the submarine's service in the Polish Navy, she was commanded by the following officers (Polish military ranks are given Soviet equivalents)[3]:

- Captain-Lieutenant (Polish: Kapitan marynarki) Władysław Janeczek: 11 April 1964 – 21 March 1966
- Captain-Lieutenant (Polish: Kapitan marynarki) Zdislaw Głowienka: 22 March 1966 – 6 November 1968
- Captain 3rd rank (Polish: Komandor podporucznik) Marian Spera: 7 November 1968 – 15 September 1970
- Captain 3rd rank (Polish: Komandor podporucznik) Józef Wołczyński: 21 July 1970 – 6 July 1975
- Captain-Lieutenant (Polish: Kapitan marynarki) Stanisław Stasik: 6 June 1975 – 31 March 1980
- Captain-Lieutenant (Polish: Kapitan marynarki) Włodzimierz Podumis: 1 April 1980 – 27 June 1985
- Captain-Lieutenant (Polish: Kapitan marynarki) Ryszard Jamro: 27 June 1985 – 15 December 1987

ORP *Kondor*

Submarine *S-358* of Project 613 was laid down on 27 July 1954, at the boathouse of the shipbuilding plant No.189 Baltic Shipyard, named after Sergo Ordzhonikidze, in the city of Leningrad. She was launched on 30 June 1955. She entered service on 12 November 1955 and on 19 November 1955 she was enlisted in the 8th Navy (from 24 December 1955 – the Red Banner Baltic Fleet) based in the city of Ust-Dvinsk (in nowadays Latvia). She was modernised in 1957 and 1960. On 7 January 1963 she was taken out of service and mothballed. She underwent a medium overhaul in the period from 4 August 1964 to 15 April 1965 for further transfer to the Polish Navy. During the repair, the snorkel and engines of the 37D model were modernised. In July 1965, the submarine made the transition from the city of Liepaja (in nowadays Latvia) to the port of Gdynia. Interestingly, the boat was initially leased to the Polish Navy, but then, in the same year, she was purchased for 3 million Polish zlotys.[4]

On 10 June 1965, the Polish flag was raised on the ship, and four days later, a ship called ORP *Kondor* (English: 'Condor') with pennant number 294 went to sea for the first time with a Polish crew. The commander was Captain-Lieutenant (Polish: Kapitan marynarki) Franciszek Wróbel and his deputy for political affairs was Captain-Lieutenant (Polish: Kapitan marynarki) Aleksev Kazimierczak. On board the ship were the commander of the Polish Navy, Vice Admiral Zdzisław Studziński and the commander of the 1st submarine brigade, Captain 1st Rank (Polish: Komandor) Henryk Pietraszkiewicz.

From 26 to 28 June 1965, the ship took part in a naval parade in the roadstead of the port of Gdynia together with units of the naval forces of the DDR and the USSR, organised on the occasion of the 20th anniversary of Victory in the Second World War.

In September of the same year, the ship conducted a series of torpedo exercises and training to overcome anti-submarine defences. These exercises began an intensive training cycle, often conducted in accordance with the principles and tactics of the Soviet Baltic Fleet.

The photograph, taken on 10 June 1965, shows the ceremony of lowering the Soviet flag and raising the Polish flag on the submarine, as well as the ceremonial formation of the first crew of the submarine. The event was attended by the commander of the Polish Navy, Vice Admiral Zdzisław Studziński. (Photo via T. Grzesikowski, C. Rudzki: ORP Kondor (294))

Another photograph taken while raising Polish flag on *Kondor*. (Photo via T. Grzesikowski, C. Rudzki: ORP Kondor (294))

In June 1966, the boat made a training campaign to the Atlantic together with classmates *Sokół* and *Bielik*, conducting joint exercises with ships of the Soviet Baltic Fleet. In June 1967 *Kondor*, along with other Polish submarines, was supposed to go on a long voyage to the Atlantic, but due to the outbreak of the Arab-Israeli Six-Day War, the expedition was cancelled and the submarine brigade was put on high alert.[5]

On 20 July 1967, the submarine detachment of the 1st Brigade began a previously planned campaign to the Atlantic, the purpose of which was to move to Murmansk, during which exercises entitled 'Submarine Operations on Enemy Communications' and 'Reconnaissance near Enemy Naval Bases' were conducted. Having passed through the Danish Straits, on 30 July, *Kondor* detected a submarine from one of the NATO countries and pursued her for some time. On 1 August, at 13.50hrs, the ship crossed the Arctic Circle, and a day later the submarine rose to the surface after 170.5 hours underwater to meet other Polish ships in the Norwegian Sea. On 5 August, the ship was ordered to cross the anti-submarine defence line guarded by ships of the Soviet Northern Fleet, which she crossed submerged, undetected by Soviet anti-submarine forces. On 8 August 1967, the ship anchored in the Murmansk roadstead, and on 21 August returned to Poland and took part in the exercises of the Warsaw Pact countries at the end of that month. In total, in 1967, the submarine spent 95 days at sea.

In February 1968, the submarine took part in the filming of the feature movie *The Last After God* (Polish: "Ostatni po Bogu") directed by Paweł Komorowski. On 17 May 1968, *Kondor*, together with her classmate *Orzeł*, set off on a trip to the North-East Atlantic for further passage to the Soviet port of Murmansk. Polish submarines practiced breaking through Soviet anti-submarine defences on the approaches to Soviet naval bases. The Polish submarines were not detected by Soviet anti-aircraft forces until they surfaced near the main base of the Soviet Northern Fleet in Murmansk. The fact that the rather outdated Polish submarines of Project 613 overcame powerful Soviet anti-submarine defences is still a matter of a legitimate pride for Polish sailors. The submarines returned to Poland on 19 June 1968, covering a distance of 4,873 nautical miles. *Kondor* during this campaign had a temporary on-board pennant number 319 to mislead the ships and aircraft of NATO countries monitoring Polish submarines.

In April 1969, the ship underwent a major overhaul at the Gdynia naval shipyard, during which, among other things, 20 square metres of light hull plating were replaced. From 9 to 18 October 1970, *Kondor* took part in Brotherhood in Arms exercises of the Warsaw Pact countries, after which she paid a friendly visit to the East German port of Rostock.[6] While going to sea from 17 to 21 August 1971, the submarine dived to a depth of 154m in the Gotland Basin. From 8 to 12 August 1972, *Kondor* took part in the Cachalot-72 exercises of the Warsaw Pact fleets. From 6 to 16 April 1973, the submarine took part in joint exercises of the navies of the USSR, Poland and the German Democratic Republic. In the first half of 1974, the ship underwent repairs at a shipyard in Gdynia. In June 1975, *Kondor* took part in the Poseidon-75 exercises of the Warsaw Pact navies, after which she underwent repairs at the shipyard in Gdynia. In 1975, the submarine was at sea for 66 days. From May 24 to May 26 1976, the boat took part in Spring-76 exercises. From 16 to 21 May 1977, *Kondor* took part in REDA-77 exercises. The ship spent a significant part of 1978 at the shipyard in Gdynia, where medium repairs were carried out and radio-electronic equipment was modernised. In particular, the Soviet 'Flag' surface target detection radar was replaced by the Polish TRN-844 radar.[7] The following year, 1979, was a very active year for the already quite outdated submarine, which spent 67 days at sea. In 1980, *Kondor* spent even more time at sea – 71 days. The gradual ageing of the ship led to the fact that by order of 12 January 1981, the maximum possible diving depth of the submarine was limited to one hundred metres; in the same year, the ship underwent another repair at the shipyard in Gdynia from 8 August to 7 September. In 1982 *Kondor* underwent a fairly lengthy repair at the MV shipyard in Gdynia, and spent only 31 days at sea. From 14 to 23 April 1983, the ship took part in exercises of the Warsaw Pact navies in the western Baltic, and from 4 to 26 May 1983, *Kondor* took part in large exercises

Kondor and the Polish minesweeper ORP *Pelikan* at sea on 20 June 1967. On this day, Polish ships discovered and lifted from the water a buoy – an automatic weather station installed by reconnaissance ships of the West Germany Navy. (Photo viaT. Grzesikowski, C. Rudzki: ORP Kondor (294))

Kondor with temporary pennant number 319 in Murmansk in early June 1968. Next to her is another Polish submarine *Orzeł*. (Photo via T. Grzesikowski, C. Rudzki: ORP Kondor (294))

Kondor at sea. (Photo via Facta_Nautica)

codenamed REDA-83. In total, in 1983, the veteran ship spent 73 days at sea. In 1984, the submarine took part in exercises REDA-84 and Barracuda-84. On 10 June 1985, on the 20th anniversary of the raising of the Polish flag, a decision was made to exclude the submarine from the lists of ships of the Polish fleet and, from that moment on, *Kondor* never went to sea again. On 30 October that the same year, the Polish flag was lowered on the ship and the ship was put into reserve. For some time, she served as a source of spare parts for the last two Project 613 submarines remaining in the Polish fleet, and after that she was dismantled for metal. During her 20 years of service in the Polish Navy, the ship covered 89,395 nautical miles – approximately 8 times more than during her previous 10 years of service in the Soviet Navy, including 19,277 miles underwater.

During the service in the Polish Navy, *Kondor* was commanded by the following officers (Polish military ranks are given Soviet equivalents):

- Captain-Lieutenant (Polish: Kapitan marynarki) Franciszek Wróbel: 25 May 1965 – 26 October 1970
- Captain-Lieutenant (Polish: Kapitan marynarki) Jerzy Gucki: 26 October 1970 – 30 September 1974
- Captain-Lieutenant (Polish: Kapitan marynarki) Wlodzimierz Mlynarczyk: 30 September 1974 – 2 October 1978
- Captain 3rd Rank (Polish: Komandor podporucznik) Eugene Chwastek: 2 October 1978 – 7 August 1981
- Captain-Lieutenant (Polish: Kapitan marynarki) Marek Ćwiklak: 7 August 1981 – 30 January 1985
- Captain-Lieutenant (Polish: Komandor podporucznik) Richard Latos: 30 January 1985 – 30 October 1985
- Lieutenant (Polish: Porucznik marynarki) Zdislaw Kasprzak: 30 October 1985 – February 1986 (date unspecified)

The first commander of *Kondor* submarine, Franciszek Wróbel, was born on 4 April 1933 in the small town of Stary Sacz (Lesser Poland Voivodeship). He graduated from the Jung School of the National Maritime Training Centre in Gdynia in 1950 and the State Maritime School in Szczecin in 1953. After that, in 1954, he was sent for military training as a backup navigator of the submarine ORP *Żbik* (French built of late 1920s). In June 1955, of his own free will, he was called up for professional service in the navy. From 19 May 1958, he served as the commander of submarine ORP *Krakowiak* (Soviet Project 96 *Malyutka*) in the 1st Submarine Brigade. In 1962-1965 he was a flag

The crew of submarine *Kondor*. (Photo via Stowarzyszenie Entuzjastów ORP Ślązak i Sympatyków Marynarki Wojennej)

The first commander of *Kondor*, Franciszek Wróbel. (Photo via https://archiwum-bhmw.wp.mil.pl)

navigator at the brigade headquarters, and then on 25 May 1965 he was appointed the commander of *Kondor*. But he gained his main reputation as the commander of a surface ship. At the end of 1970, he was transferred to the Navy Hydrographic Protection Directorate as the first commander of the new ship ORP *Kopernik*, a Polish hydrographic ship of Project 861 (NATO reporting name: *Moma*-class). In 1975, *Kopernik*, under the command of Wróbel, together with Polish specialised research institutes carried out geophysical research on the bottom of the southern Baltic Sea, which led to the discovery of oil and natural gas fields in the economic zone of Poland. In December 1976, Franciszek Wróbel and many other specialists of the Polish Navy took part in a polar expedition, combined with the construction of the Henryk Arctowski polar station of the Polish Academy of Sciences, in Antarctica. In 1976 and 1978, *Kopernik*, under the command of Wróbel, made expeditions to Spitsbergen with a scientific group of the Polish Academy of Sciences. Another task assigned to the commander of *Kopernik* was a polar expedition to Antarctica with a total duration of 125 days. The expedition began on 1 December 1979, and the equator was crossed on 17 December. On board the ship during this expedition were scientists from the Institute of Geophysics of the Polish Academy of Sciences, the Institute of Geophysics of the AGH University of Science and Technology in Krakow, and the company 'Marine and Terrestrial Geophysics' from Toruń. Scientists from Argentina joined these foreign teams. Commander Franciszek Wróbel also acted as deputy leader in this expedition. On 31 December 1979, *Kopernik* arrived at Henryk Arctowski station on King George Island, where she conducted seismic studies of the seabed in the area of King George Island and Bransfield Strait, as well as in the South Shetland Islands, in Drake Passage, and in the Antarctic Peninsula area, in the Gerlach Strait and in the Palmer Archipelago. The main focus of the work was the study of the earth's crust and upper mantle in the selected region. The ship returned to Gdynia on 4 April 1980, after 125 days of sailing, during which she covered 23,157 nautical miles. Franciszek Wróbel commanded *Kopernik* until 2 June 1986, after which he retired and settled permanently in his hometown of Stary Sacz. He was the author of several textbooks on navigation and celestial navigation, published from 1968 to the present. His *Sea Voyage. Tasks with Explanations* (Polish: *Nawigacja morska. Zadania z objaśnieniami*), *Deck Officer's Handbook* (Polish: *Vademecum oficera wachtowego*) and *Navigator's Handbook* (Polish: *Vademecum nawigatora*) have been the basis of maritime literature for many years and play a huge role in training maritime personnel of the Republic of Poland. Franciszek Wróbel was awarded the Officer's and Knight's Crosses of the Order of the Renaissance of Poland (Polish: Oficerskim i Kawalerskim Orderu Odrodzenia Polski), the gold badge 'Exemplary Commander' (Polish: 'Wzorowy Dowódca'), as well as the gold and silver badge 'Honored Naval Activist' (Polish: 'Zasłużony Pracownik Morza'). He died on 27 July 2022.[8]

ORP *Bielik*

Submarine *S-279* of Project 613 was laid down on 20 July 1954, at the boathouse of the shipbuilding plant No.112 Krasnoe Sormovo, named after. A.A. Zhdanov, in the city of Gorky (nowadays Nizhny Novgorod). She was launched on 23 April 1955. In May 1955, she was transferred via the internal water communications system of the USSR to Leningrad to undergo acceptance tests. The boat was commissioned on 20 October 1955 and on 31 October she became a part of the 4th Navy (from 24 December 1955 – the Red Banner Baltic Fleet). By 1 December 1956 the submarine had been taken out of service and mothballed in the harbour of the city of Paldiski (nowadays a part of Estonia). On 15 July 1961 she was reactivated, went into operation and was based in the city of Ust-Dvinsk (nowadays a part of Latvia). On 7 July 1963, the submarine was again taken out of service and mothballed in the harbour of the city of Paldiski. On 15 April 1964 she was once again reactivated and based in the city of Ust-Dvinsk. Soon after reactivation, preparations began for the transfer of the boat to the Polish Navy. In June 1965, the submarine made the transition from the city of Liepaja (nowadays a part of Latvia) to the port of Gdynia. On 1 July, the Polish flag was raised on the ship, the submarine became a part of the Polish fleet under the name ORP *Bielik* (English: 'White-tailed Eagle') and received pennant number 295.

From 4 to 11 November 1965, together with *Orzeł*, she carried out training missions in the southern Baltic. From 28 June 1966 to 29 July 1966, the submarine was on an autonomous cruise in the North Sea and North-East Atlantic with two other Polish *Whiskeys*: *Kondor* and *Sokół*.

On 11 June 1967, *Bielik*, along with other Polish submarines, was placed on high alert in connection with the Israeli-Arab Six Day War. She was given the task of entering the Baltic Sea. After returning to port, the crew

Bielik with temporary pennant number 311 in Murmansk, in August 1967. (Photo via Stowarzyszenie Entuzjastów ORP Ślązak i Sympatyków Marynarki Wojennej)

began preparing the ship for passage to the Atlantic with a visit to the Soviet port of Murmansk. This ocean campaign lasted from 20 July to 21 August 1967. In addition to *Bielik*, three other Polish submarines took part in it – classmates of Project 613: *Sokół*, *Kondor* and *Orzeł*. *Bielik*, on the way to Murmansk, had a temporary pennant number 311.

In May 1968, together with submarine *Sęp* (pre-war Dutch built), she visited the East German port of Rostock.

From 10 September 1970 to 8 October 1970, the boat, together with *Sokół*, was on a combat training campaign in the North-East Atlantic. In 1971, she was transferred to the Submarine Division of the 3rd Flotilla of warships of the PPR Navy with the same location. From 1 to 11 October 1974, together with two other Polish *Whiskeys* – *Kondor* and *Sokół* – the submarine was on a friendly visit to the DDR.

In June 1975, the ship took part in exercises codenamed Poseidon-75. In October 1975, *Bielik* received the title of 'Leading Ship of the Fleet'.

From 4 to 26 May 1983, the ship took part in large naval exercises codenamed Reda-83. In 1985 the submarine underwent another repair at the shipyard in Gdynia.

On 29 September 1988, *Bielik* was withdrawn from service in the Polish Navy. Later she was dismantled in Świnoujście.

It is interesting to note that in the late 1960s Leszek Cezary Miller, the Prime Minister of Poland in 2001-2004, served on *Bielik*.

Bielik is the only Polish *Whiskey* for which the author did not find complete information about her commanders. Therefore, the given list is incomplete and requires further research. During the submarine *Bielik's* service in the Polish Navy, she was commanded by the following officers (Polish military ranks are given Soviet equivalents):

- Captain-Lieutenant (Polish: Kapitan marynarki) Józef Węgrzyn: from mid-1965 (according to other data from 12 November 1966) – to 1969
- Captain Kocyk – no dates nor details on rank known
- Captain-Lieutenant (Polish: Kapitan marynarki) Henryk Kula – no dates known
- Deputy Commander of the Polish navy in 2000 Admiral Jędrzej Czajkowski was the deputy commander of the submarine and then her commander in 1975-1977
- Captain 3rd Rank (Polish: Komandor podporucznik) Edward Olewiński – no dates known
- Captain Bryda – no dates nor details on rank known
- Captain-Lieutenant (Polish: Kapitan marynarki) Ryszard Latos – no dates known
- Captain-Lieutenant (Polish: Kapitan marynarki) Ryszard Jamro: 1987-1988

Polish naval officer Jozef Wegrzyn began serving in the navy on 18 November 1952. During his nearly thirty-year career, he passed through virtually every level of command, from sailor to full commander. In January 1953, he entered the School of Naval Specialists, where he received basic maritime training. Two years later he began studying at the Naval Officer School at the naval department. After graduation, he devoted his entire future career to submarines. On 1 October 1958, he joined the 1st Submarine Brigade and took the position of commander of the combat navigation and communications department on submarine ORP *Kurp* (Soviet Project 96 *Malyutka*). By 16 October 1959, he was an assistant commander of *Kurp*. On 30 December 1962, he became a deputy commander of the submarine ORP *Orzeł*, where he served until April 1965. Then in mid-1965 (according to other data from 12 November 1966) with the rank of Lieutenant-Commander, he became the commander of ORP *Bielik*. Three years later he became a senior assistant of Chief of Staff of the 1st Submarine Brigade. In April 1971 he was transferred to the Navy headquarters. By July 1972 he was in command of a submarine

ORP *Bielik* (to the right) in Rostock, in 1968. (Photo via Stowarzyszenie Entuzjastów ORP Ślązak i Sympatyków Marynarki Wojennej)

Bielik in Hel, in 1974. (Photo via Stowarzyszenie Entuzjastów ORP Ślązak i Sympatyków Marynarki Wojennej)

Bielik at sea. (Photo via Stowarzyszenie Entuzjastów ORP Ślązak i Sympatyków Marynarki Wojennej)

Bielik during a naval parade in 1976. Near her (to the left) is the classmate *Kondor*. (Photo via Kazimierz Gosz)

squadron, already having been promoted to Captain-Lieutenant. In 1974, acknowledging his service excellence, he was included in the 'Honorary Book of Military Feats' (Polish: 'Honorowa Księga Czynów Żołnierskich'). He ended his Navy career on 6 September 1980.[9] Died on 25 July 2008.

Concluding the story about the service of Project 613 submarines in the Polish Navy, first of all it needs noting the excellent condition and combat readiness of the Polish submarines. According to the author's subjective assessment, Polish *Whiskeys* were the most battle-ready ships of this project in all foreign navies and, at least, were not inferior to their Soviet peers on the ships of Project 613. Despite the rather late arrival of four *Whiskeys* to the Polish Navy, the ships completed their service perfectly. The spectacular breakthrough of the Soviet anti-submarine defences in the Murmansk area in 1968 perfectly demonstrated that in the event of a conflict with NATO in the 1960-70s, the outdated but well-prepared Polish Project 613 submarines would have created a serious headache for the anti-submarine forces of the North Atlantic Bloc. Separately, it is worth noting the excellent work of the Stocznia Marynarki Wojennej (MW) shipyard in Gdynia in repairing and modernising these submarines.

Repairs of *Bielik* in 1985. (Photo via Stowarzyszenie Entuzjastów ORP Ślązak i Sympatyków Marynarki Wojennej)

Loading torpedoes onto *Bielik* in 1980. (Photo via Stowarzyszenie Entuzjastów ORP Ślązak i Sympatyków Marynarki Wojennej)

A group of the Polish submarine officers. Third from the right (in coat) is the commander of *Bielik*, Captain-Lieutenant Józef Wegrzyn. (Photo via Tadeusz Czeczot family album)

Left: Leszek Caesar Miller during service on *Bielik*. (Photo courtesy Jan Iwaszczyszyn/Facebook)

Centre: First commander of Bielik, Józef Węgrzyn. (Photo via Stowarzyszenie Entuzjastów ORP Ślązak i Sympatyków Marynarki Wojennej)

Right: Coat of arms of *Bielik*. (Photo via Stowarzyszenie Entuzjastów ORP Ślązak i Sympatyków Marynarki Wojennej)

Polish submarines of Project 613 in Murmansk in 1967. (Photo via Stowarzyszenie Entuzjastów ORP Ślązak i Sympatyków Marynarki Wojennej)

9

MISSING WHISKEYS OF THE SYRIAN NAVY

The history of the service of Project 613 submarines in the Syrian Navy is the most mysterious and little-studied topic. It leaves more questions than answers, and also makes us sincerely regret the little interest of official Soviet sources and historians in studying the service and fate of 'made in the USSR' weapons abroad. Until now, various sources do not have a clear and unified understanding of both the number of submarines of this project delivered to Syria or their fate. The most common information in the modern Russian blogosphere about *Whiskeys* in Syria is data on the delivery in 1959 of three submarines, *S-167, S-171* and *S-183*, to the Syrian part of the UAR (United Arab Republic). The most complete information about the possible fate of Soviet submarines in the Syrian fleet (if this notion could be applied to the minimum data on the issue under consideration) is provided by the famous researcher of the supply of Soviet naval equipment abroad, Alexander Rozin.[1]

Let us recall once again that on 22 February 1958, Egypt and Syria united into a single United Arab Republic, but arms supply continued to be carried out separately for both the Egyptian and Syrian armies. It is obvious that payment also came separately from each of the united states. The contract for the supply of three *Whiskeys*, two minesweepers and six torpedo boats to Syria was concluded in the first half of 1958, and it was not the Egyptian part of the UAR that paid for the ships, but Syrian. Submarines for the Syrians were supplied from the 37th separate Red Banner Submarine Brigade of the Baltic Fleet. Here is a brief look at the pre-Arab career of each of the submarines.

Submarine *S-167* of Project 613 was laid down on 13 June 1953, at the boathouse of the shipbuilding plant No.112 Krasnoye Sormovo, named after A.A. Zhdanov, in the city of Gorky (nowadays Nizhny Novgorod). She was launched on 5 November 1953. She was transferred down the Volga and Caspian Sea to the plant's acceptance base in the city of Baku to undergo acceptance tests, and in the spring of 1954, she was transferred via the inland water systems of the USSR to the city of Leningrad. The boat entered service on 30 July 1954, and on 7 August 1954 she was included in the 4th Navy (from 24 December 1955 – the Red Banner Baltic Fleet).

Submarine *S-171* of Project 613 was laid down on 8 September 1953, at the boathouse of the shipbuilding plant No.112 Krasnoye Sormovo, named after A.A. Zhdanov, in the city of Gorky (nowadays Nizhny Novgorod). She was launched on 30 December 1953. She was transferred in May 1954 to Leningrad to undergo acceptance tests. Entering service on 10 August 1954, on 17 August she was included in the 4th Navy (from 24 December 1955 – the Red Banner Baltic Fleet).

Submarine *S-167* in the Merchant Harbor of Kronstadt, July 1955. (Photo via archive of I. Mironova through http://www.ruspodplav.ru)

Submarine *S-183* of Project 613 was laid down on 15 February 1954, at the boathouse of the shipbuilding plant No.112 Krasnoye Sormovo, named after A.A. Zhdanov, in the city of Gorky (nowadays Nizhny Novgorod). She was launched on 9 June 1954. In the summer of 1954, she was transferred down the Volga and Caspian Sea to the plant's acceptance base in the city of Baku to undergo acceptance tests. The submarine entered service on 14 December 1954, and, in the summer of 1955, was transferred via the inland water systems of the USSR from Baku to the city of Leningrad. Commissioned on 20 September 1955, she became a part of the 4th Navy (from 24 December 1955 – the Red Banner Baltic Fleet).

Regarding the transfer of boats to the Syrians, on 22 January 1959, a US intelligence bulletin reported that "Three Soviet *Whiskey*-class submarines and a T43-class minesweeper, which left the Baltic Sea on January 7, have moved to the eastern Mediterranean." On 26 to 27 January 1959, American and European newspapers published a short note that the Egyptian fleet received three more *Whiskey* submarines from USSR. However, the Soviet Union did not transfer any submarines to the Egyptians in 1959. At this time, relations between the USSR and Egypt sharply deteriorated due to the campaign launched in December 1958 in the UAR against the Egyptian and Syrian communists. As a result of this development, Soviet military assistance to Egypt was temporarily suspended. The three mentioned submarines were intended for the Syrian Navy, which was a part of the United Arab Republic. They were paid for by the Syrian government. On 17 February 1959, *S-167*, *S-171* and *S-183* were decommissioned from the Soviet Navy due to the sale to the Syrian Navy.

All three boats of Project 613 were based in Egyptian ports and were supposed to train Syrian crews. However, everything that then happened was contrary to the expectations of the Syrian sailors. Initially, the submarines were commanded by Syrian Lieutenant Colonel Mustafa Shahin, but after some time the Egyptians removed him from command of the formation of these submarines and appointed an Egyptian officer in his place. Next, the Egyptians demanded that the Syrians pay the costs of maintaining the submarines. The materials of the Cultural Research and Documentation Centre in Sidon include information from the Syrian Department of Foreign Affairs, which reveals Syrian data about how unification with Egypt took place in 1958-1961 in the armed forces. The issue with submarines was not ignored there either:

> Regarding submarines, I would like to mention that with the formation of the detachment, the Egyptians decided to station Syrian submarines in Alexandria under the pretext that there was no matching port in Syria and that the naval training of these units could be to unite and educate Syrians and Egyptians together. These submarines remained throughout the unit's stay in Alexandria, and no Syrians were allowed to train on them. At the end of the days of unity, the leadership of the Egyptian Navy sent a statement to the leadership of the First Army for 10 million Syrian pounds – the cost of maintaining, repairing Syrian submarines and fuel, even though the submarines had become expendable.

On 26 September 1961, a group of Syrian officers carried out a coup in Syria, and Damascus seceded from the UAR. So the question arises: in the coup's aftermath, where did the three Syrian submarines previously based in Egypt go?

Initially, the Egyptians kept them. In the diary of Akram Zuaiter (published in 2021), who was in 1963-1964 a Jordanian Ambassador in Damascus, an entry dated 15 October 1962 states that "Gamal Abdel Nasser captured Syria's most important weapons…He also captured three submarines that Syria bought with its own money…".

What happened further to *S-167*, *S-171* and *S-183* is still not clear. One version of events can be assumed to be that the Syrian boats were used to supply Egyptian boats with spare parts, and one of them could even have been used as a donor for the submarine launched by the Egyptians. Moshe Shai's book *Aḥi 'Elat': goralah shel mashḥetet*, written after the Six-Day War of 1967, provides the following interesting information:

> The Egyptian Navy currently has 12 Ocean submarines… Of the 12 Egyptian submarines, two belong to The Syrian Navy, which were transferred to the Egyptian Navy during the Egyptian-Syrian Union and remained in its hands even after the collapse. Syria demanded the return of these two submarines, but Egypt evaded and has not yet responded to the requests of the Syrian fleet.

As previously mentioned, the Egyptian resource 'group73historians.com', in an article devoted to Egyptian submarines, confirms 7 *Whiskey*-class boats in different states of readiness before the start of Yom Kippur War.[2] Only five of them were directly supplied by Soviets. There is no further mention of the eventual fate of the three ex-Soviet submarines, nor is there any data on how actively the Egyptians used them in their navy. We remember that the training of crews and repairs of Project 613 submarines took place with active Soviet participation, and it is unlikely that Soviet comrades would help Egyptian sailors with maintaining combat readiness of submarines captured from no less friendly Syria.

Authoritative Western sources generally go further and do not mention that the Syrians had the three described submarines (formally, this is so, because the boats were part of the UAR Navy and were never formally given to Syria). The Syrians did, however, receive their *Whiskey*. But it was no longer a full-fledged attack submarine, rather, as in the case of the Cuban Navy, a submarine converted into a charging and training station. She was intended to serve three Soviet submarines of Project 633 (NATO reporting name: *Romeo*-class) delivered to the Syrian Navy between 1986 and 1987. According to the recollections of the commander and instructor of one of the Syrian *Romeo*, Vladimir Alekseevich Anikin, the delivery of the training *Whiskey* took place in the spring of 1987, this boat was commanded by Lieutenant Commander Viktor Yakovlevich Don. The 1991 *Jane's Fighting Ships* handbook gives other clearly erroneous information: 'One ex-Soviet *Whiskey*-class submarine transferred from the Black Sea in November 1985 and operates as an auxiliary charging platform.'

Indirect confirmation of the transfer of a charging and training *Whiskey* submarine to the Syrians is the awarding of a certificate from the Minister of Defence of Syria in July 2017 to Ivan Vasilyevich Matveev, who transferred the submarine to the Syrian Navy in the period 1986 to 1988. It is indicated that he served on Project 613 submarines and was an electrician with the rank of senior midshipman.[3] Thus, the words of V.A. Anikin about the transfer of the submarine in 1987 are confirmed. Unfortunately, the author does not have information about the initial pennant number of the Soviet submarine, rebuilt into a training and charging facility and transferred to Syria.

Lieutenant-Commander Viktor Yakovlevich Don, commander of the training *Whiskey* boat transferred to Syria. Lieutenant-Commander Don gained fame in 1983 as the head of the emergency rescue service of the rescue ship *SS-21* of the Soviet Black Sea Fleet, which participated in the study of the submarine *Shch-204* that was lost off the coast of Bulgaria during the Second World War. As of 1983, he had logged 2,100 hours under water. (Photo via Gangut Publishing House)

As far as is known, the service of the outdated *Romeos* in the Syrian Navy was short-lived and in the late 1990s the boats no longer went to sea. Obviously, the need for the charging/training *Whiskey* also disappeared. Fortunately, photographs of the Syrian *Whiskey* taken around 2005 have been preserved: subsequently, the Syrian *Romeos* and *Whiskey* were scrapped.

Conclusion

The information disclosed in this book gives a fairly complete picture of the role that Project 613 submarines played in the development of the navies of those countries where they were in service. In most cases, we can say that this role was exceptional. For example, Indonesia, which gained independence only in 1945, by the early 1960s had become the leading maritime power in South and Southeast Asia, while the *Whiskey*-class submarines became the most dangerous combat component of the Jakarta fleet for its neighbours. The Indonesian president and the fleet commands without the slightest hesitation sent submarines to the different parts of the world: from Karachi to the island of Timor, from the western shores of Australia to the Philippines. Perhaps very often it looked like a bluff, but it produced results: the Dutch gave up Western New Guinea, the Indians accelerated negotiations with Pakistan to resolve the 1965 conflict, and so on. Another example is China, which, having launched its own production of *Whiskey* submarines, immediately gained advantage over the Taiwanese fleet, levelling the superiority (at that time) in the surface ships of the Kuomintang. Whether it is a coincidence or not, after the Chinese Navy adopted 21 new Type 6603 submarines, naval skirmishes with the Taiwanese fleet almost ceased. Egypt stands apart, whilst having a large submarine fleet managed to instil fear in its neighbours, it was unable to realise its potential. Very little is known about the use of four Project 613 submarines by the DPRK fleet, but they were the founders of the country's now countless submarine fleet. Tiny

The submarine of Project 633 and the training *Whiskey*, withdrawn from the Syrian Navy, in the port of Tartus. (Tom Cooper collection)

Albania, having even broken ties with the USSR, boldly threatened Italy with its four *Whiskeys*. Bulgaria, having received two Project 613 submarines, was for the first time able to operate throughout the Black Sea and not be afraid of any Turkish warship. Poland also stands apart. The author believes that the maintenance and use of Project 613 submarines by the Poles was close to ideal. The submarines were used by the Polish Navy many times more intensively than in the Soviet fleet, but the reliability of the submarines of this project and timely repairs allowed them to complete 20 years of service in *Marynarka Wojenna* without serious accidents.

Whiskeys' service in foreign navies allowed us to take a different look at the common beliefs about the noisiness and obsolescence of the submarines. The Indonesian *Whiskeys* successfully hid from the sonars of quite modern frigates of the Australian and Pakistani navies and, according to the Indonesian sources, the surfacing of submarine *Alugoro* near the British aircraft carrier *Victorious* on 12 September 1964 was also a complete surprise for the British. The story of an easy breakthrough by Polish Project 613 submarines of the Soviet anti-submarine defences system near Murmansk during the exercises in 1968 speaks for itself.

The history of the combat use of submarines of the project under consideration requires a separate discussion. Indonesian submarines were used to land saboteurs in Dutch-controlled territory in 1962, with at least two of them coming under attack by Dutch warships and aircraft. Indonesian boats were damaged, but at the same time skilfully avoided attacks. This is especially important considering that by the time of the famous expedition to land Indonesian special forces, the submarines had only been in service with the Indonesian Navy for six months and the crews may not have yet fully mastered the submarines. On the contrary, *Whiskeys* of the Egyptian Navy could not prove themselves in any way. And if the lack of reliable victories over Israeli surface ships can still be explained by the small size of the Israeli fleet as such or by the quality of Soviet torpedoes – low-speed guided Soviet torpedoes SAET-50, made on the basis of the German T-5 from the Second World War, or unguided 53-51 could hardly have been a serious threat to the Israeli Navy. But why the Israel's main seaports were not littered with mines over the years (especially during the long War of Attrition) remains a big question. Several hundred AMD-1000 mines deployed from Egyptian *Whiskeys* could have radically changed the situation with the economic blockade of Israel. In addition to Indonesia and Egypt, Project 613 boats could theoretically have been used by the PRC and DPRK navies during clashes with the fleets of Taiwan and South Korea, respectively, but there is no evidence of this.

The attached table provides condensed general information on the countries that used Project 613 submarines:

Project 613 class was the second widespread type of Soviet-designed submarine that served abroad, 'losing' only to Project 633 submarines (NATO reporting name: *Romeo*-class). However, we note that most of the *Whiskeys* were Soviet-made and supplied directly from the USSR, while more than 100 *Romeos* were mainly produced in China and North Korea. It is interesting that no other type of Soviet submarines has ever achieved such export figures; even *Varshavyankas* of Project 877 and Project 636 (NATO reporting name: *Kilo*-class), which were extremely successful in the export markets, fall slightly short of the export numbers of *Whiskeys*.

When writing this book, the author set himself several goals, which he hopes were achieved during the course of the story:

Firstly, to solve the problem of introducing the general reader to an important page in the history of Soviet military shipbuilding and the export of submarines. The topic of the service of Soviet submarines in foreign fleets (both Project 613 in particular and other types of submarines in general) is well known to navy enthusiasts, but for some reason does not receive the wide popularity it deserves.

Secondly, to show that, despite the fact that the submarines in question were not the best ships in the world in their class and were often equipped with simplified export mechanisms, with the proper level of maintenance and crew training, they could successfully carry out the combat missions assigned to them. The Indonesian *Whiskeys* service is a brilliant confirmation of this postulate.

Thirdly, to debunk the myth that Soviet technology is unreliable and cannot last long. The best refutation of this myth is the Polish *Whiskeys* service. One of the keys to their successful operation was timely repairs.

Fourthly, to acquaint readers with little-known (sometimes not covered at all in Russian literature) facts about the service of ships, the careers of their commanders and other remarkable related events.

And the last but not the least important task is aesthetic perception. Almost two hundred, often rare, photographs of *Whiskeys* in service with foreign navies provide an opportunity to admire their beautiful forms.

At the same time, for the sake of objectivity, it should be noted that a number of facts and events related to the service of Project 613 submarines in foreign navies remained incompletely disclosed, largely due to the lack of relevant information in the public domain. There is catastrophically little information about the service of Egyptian and, especially, North Korean submarines. The mystery of the fate of the three Syrian boats has not been solved; quite informative Chinese sources are stingy with information about the service and fate of submarines of Type 6603. All this leaves enormous opportunities for new research and works within the framework of the topic.

Operating navy	Number of submarines	Notes
Albania	4	
Bulgaria	2	
Egypt	10 supplied from USSR + 3 captured from Syrians	5 were returned to USSR after the end of the leasing period
Indonesia	12	
China	21	Made in China as Type 6603
North Korea	4	
Cuba	1	Floating Charging Station
Poland	4	
Syria	4 (3 of them captured by Egyptians and never used by the Syrian Navy)	One of the supplied boats was a Floating Charging Station
Total:	**62**	

BIBLIOGRAPHY

Батаршев А.В., Дубивко А.Ф., Любимов В.С. «Карибский кризис глазами российских подводников. (пятьдесят пять лет спустя)» 2017 г.

Безик И.В., «Советско-индонезийское военно-морское сотрудничество», статья

Бережной С. С. «Подводные лодки России и СССР», рукопись

Жданкин Андрей «Неизвестный поход советских моряков в Индонезию», 2011 г.

Заблоцкий В.П., Подводные лодки проекта 613. Морская коллекция. 2014.

Козлов В. «Подводная война. Горизонты великого противостояния сверхдержав». М. Яуза, Эксмо 2005 г.

Козлов В. Контр-адмирал в отставке «Тогда в Албании.» Журнал «Морской сборник», № 6, 1994 г.

Кузин В.П., Никольский В.И. «Военно-Морской Флот СССР 1945-1991», СПб,. Историческое Морское Общество, 653 с., 1996

Лебедько В.Г. «Верность долгу» Санкт-Петербург, «Развитие», 2005 г.

Мозговой А. Великолепные 613-е // Военный парад : журнал. — 2001. — Ноябрь-декабрь (т. 48, № 06), ISSN 1029-4678

Подводные лодки 613 проекта. Альманах «Корабли и сражения», 2002.

Попов А. В., «Экономика Индонезии: современное состояние и тенденции развития», Федеральное государственное бюджетное учреждение науки Институт востоковедения РАН Институт стран Востока, Москва, 2019

Постнов А.А. Модернизация подводных лодок проекта 613, ВТС Бастион, №2, 2000

Рыжиков Р. В. На румбе – океан / Р. В. Рыжиков. – СПб.: Новик, 2004

Тарас А. Е. «Дизельные подводные лодки 1950-2005», Харвест, 2006, ISBN 5-17-036930-1.

Титушкин С. И. – Подводные лодки 613 проекта.

Черчилль Р.С. и У. Шестидневная война. — Иерусалим, «Библиотека-Алия», 1989

Ходжа Э. «Хрущевцы.» Воспоминания. — Тирана: «8 Нентори», 1980. — 515 с.

Шаломов В., Тимохин И. Подводные лодки проекта 613 амурских корабелов. // Морской сборник. — 2022. — № 12.

English language books and magazines:

Ashraf Refaat, 'The Egyptian Navy in the 1973 October War', *Naval Forces* Vol. XIX, No.5/1998

Ashraf Refaat, 'Naval aspects of the 1967 War', *Al-Ahram Weekly*, 7 May 2013

Chaim Herzog, *War of Atonement. The Inside Story of the Yom Kippur War*, (Casemate: First Edition, 2010)

China Files, Peoples Liberation Army Navy Ships, Fact Sheet, ADF Issue, Weapons Systems Brief., Pub: Time of Flight, Media Department. ADF V.2.1 RESEARCH SHEETS, Kerry Plowright 2008

Edgar O'Balance, *No Victor, No Vanquished: The Yom Kippur War*, (Presidio Pr: Reprint edition, 1991)

Gardiner, Robert, *Conway's all the World's Fighting Ships 1947-1995* (Annapolis, MD: Naval Institute Press, 1995)

George S. Dragnich, *THE SOVIET UNION'S QUEST FOR ACCESS TO NAVAL FACILITIES IN EGYPT PRIOR TO THE JUNE WAR OF 1967*, (Center for Naval Analyses Arlington, Virginia, July 1974)

Jane's Fighting Ships 1961-1962 (The McGraw-Hill Book Company, Inc., 1961)

Jane's Fighting Ships 1962-1963 (Sampson Low, First Edition, 1963)

Jane's Fighting Ships 1967-1968 (Potter Row, 1st edition, 1968)

Jane's Fighting Ships, 1972-73, 75th Year of Issue (Mcgraw-Hill, First American Edition, 1972)

John Moore, ed., *Jane's Fighting Ships by John Moore (Editor), 1973-1974 Edition* (McGraw – Hill, 1973)

Moore, Captain John E., ed., *Jane's Fighting Ships 1974-1975* (Watts, 1975)

Moore, John, ed., *Jane's Fighting Ships 1976-77* (Macdonald & Jane's, 1976., 1st American Edition 1976)

Moore, John, *Jane's Fighting Ships 1978-79* (Jane's Publishing Co Ltd, First Edition, 1978)

Klaus Mommsen, *60 YEARS ISRAEL NAVY: Chel Ha'Yam Ha'Yisraeli*, (Books on Demand; ISBN-10: 3842349068; ISBN-13: 978-3842349063. April 2011)

Polmar, Norman & Noot, Jurrien, *Submarines of the Russian and Soviet Navies, 1718–1990*, (Annapolis, Maryland: Naval Institute Press, 1991)

'LATEST SOVIET ARMS DELIVERY TO SYRIA', 4 October 1957, Current Intelligence Bulletin, www.cia.gov

Bulgarian language books and magazines:

Николай ЙОРДАНОВ, Димитър ВЪРБАНОВ, «ПРЕДИ 60 ГОДИНИ – В БОЙНИЯ СТРОЙ НА БЪЛГАРСКИТЕ ВМС ПОСТЪПВАТ НА ВЪОРЪЖЕНИЕ ПОДВОДНИЦИ ОТ ПРОЕКТ 613», Морски Вестник

Indonesian language books and magazines:

"Jalesveva Jayamahe", Dipersembahkan oleh: Djawatan Penerangan Angkatan Laut, Achir Tahun, 1960

Polish language books and magazines:

Czesław Rudzki: ORP «Orzeł» (292)

Henryk Sołkiewicz (red.): Ewolucyjny rozwój sił okrętowych Marynarki Wojennej w latach 1945–2010. Gdynia: Wydawnictwo BP/Akademia Marynarki Wojennej, 2015

Marek Soroka. Polskie okręty wojenne 1945-1980. Wydawn. Morskie, 1986, ISBN 978-83-215-3249-3.

Robert Rochowicz. Reda-83 – kiedyś to były ćwiczenia. „Morze, Statki i Okręty». Nr 7-8 (1999), 2020. Magnum-X. ISSN 1426-529X

Tadeusz Grzesikowski, Czesław Rudzki: ORP Orzeł [292], w: „Morza, Statki i Okręty» nr 5/1998

Tadeusz Grzesikowski, Czesław Rudzki, ORP Sokół [293], „Morza, Statki i Okręty» nr 2/3, 1999, ISSN 1426-529X.

Tadeusz Grzesikowski, Czesław Rudzki. ORP Kondor (294). „Morza, Statki i Okręty». 3, 2000. ISSN 1426-529x

Zbigniew Damski. ORP Orzeł. Dom Wydawniczy Bellona, 2000. ISBN 978-83-11-09106-1

Internet resources used for collecting information and photographs:

http://alerozin.narod.ru; https://archiwum-bhmw.wp.mil.pl; https://amw.gdynia.pl; http://artofwar.ru; https://www.beritatrans.com; https://bhmw.wp.mil.pl; https://www.bilibili.com; www.blackseavisits.ru; http://blog.sina.com.cn; https://bulevardionline.com; http://www.china.org.cn; https://coollib.com; http://cpc.people.com.cn; www.deepstorm.ru; http://defense-studies.blogspot.com; https://defencehub.live; https://www.defencetalk.com; https://www.detik.com; https://dewey.petra.ac.id; https://durreslajm.al; www.facebook.com; https://flot.com; http://forums.airbase.ru; https://forum.axishistory.com; https://www.france24.com; https://www.indonesiamandiri.web.id; https://www.indomiliter.com; https://intisari.grid.id; http://garudamiliter.blogspot.com; https://www.goodnewsfromindonesia.id; http://www.kartonwork.pl; https://www.kchf.ru; https://koarmada2.tnial.mil.id; https://kodiklatal.tnial.mil.id; https://www.kommersant.ru; https://lenta.ru; https://www.livejournal.com; https://manado.tribunnews.com; https://www.masress.com; www.medialb.com; https://www.merdeka.com; https://military.wikireading.ru; http://militaryrussia.ru; http://militera.lib.ru; https://morskivestnik.com; http://mil.news.sina.com.cn; www.mw.mil.pl; https://nationalinterest.org; https://naval-encyclopedia.com; www.news.com.au; https://news.detik.com; https://www.noemamag.com; https://www.nytimes.com; www.outono.net; https://www.pan.bg; https://pbc.gda.pl; www.pelasgoskoritsas.gr; http://politics.people.com.cn; https://polska-org.pl; http://www.primeportal.net; http://qdsq.qingdao.gov.cn; https://www.radarmiliter.com; https://radhima.files.wordpress.com; https://www.rediff.com; https://www.reuters.com; http://www.ruspodplav.ru; https://russian7.ru; https://www.sinodefenceforum.com; http://slide.mil.news.sina.com.cn; https://www.smartage.pl; https://sot.com.al; https://www.shqiperia.com; www.submariners-bg.com; https://telegraf.al; https://top-channel.tv; https://www.usinflationcalculator.com; http://www.vetsubmlat.narod.ru; http://vimpel.boinaslava.net; http://weaponstechnology.blogspot.com; http://www.xinhuanet.com; http://xn--b1atgapb.xn--p1ai; https://zbiam.pl; https://zhuanlan.zhihu.com

ENDNOTES

Chapter 1

1 'Edip Ohri: E vërteta për nëndetëset shqiptare', *Gazeta Telegraf*, 28 July 2018.
2 'Создание советской базы ВМФ в Албании.' https://el-tolstyh.livejournal.com/348233.html
3 'Как в 1961 году Албания отобрала у СССР 4 подводные лодки».' https://russian7.ru/post/kak-v-1961-godu-albaniya-otobrala-u-sssr-4-pod/
4 'Это наивное пиратство.' https://www.kommersant.ru/doc/4814899
5 'Jak Mandrea dhe historia e sabotazheve ruse me nëndetëset shqiptare.' https://durreslajm.al/jak-mandrea-dhe-historia-e-sabotazheve-ruse-me-nendeteset-shqiptare/
6 'Mardheniet Shqiptaro-Sovjetike ne bazen detare te Vlore.' https://www.shqiperia.com/Mardheniet-Shqiptaro-Sovjetike-ne-bazen-detare-te-Vlore.16306/
7 Романов B.A., 'Несокрушимая и легендарная: Албанская народная армия.' Часть 5 http://artofwar.ru/s/shatxko_s_w/text_1630.shtml
8 'DETARIA SHQIPTARE NË RRJEDHËN E KOHËS', стр 226, https://radhima.files.wordpress.com/2019/11/detaria-shqiptare_libri-i-faqosur.pdf
9 Романов B.A,. 'Несокрушимая и легендарная: Албанская народная армия.' Часть 5 http://artofwar.ru/s/shatxko_s_w/text_1630.shtml
10 'Albania's Soviet-era sub awaits its fate, refusing to sink.' https://www.france24.com/en/live-news/20220518-albania-s-soviet-era-sub-awaits-its-fate-refusing-to-sink
11 'Albania to sell Soviet-made submarines for scrap.' https://www.reuters.com/article/idINIndia-46663220100304
12 'Three of four submarines for scrap metal.' https://top-channel.tv/english/three-of-four-submarines-for-scrap-metal/
13 'Nëndetëset përfundojnë në Elbasan.' https://top-channel.tv/2011/09/24/nendeteset-perfundojne-ne-elbasan/
14 'Durrsaku Xhemal Shani, Komandanti i Parë i Brigadës së Nëndetëseve Shqiptare.' https://bulevardionline.com/durrsaku-xhemal-shani-komandanti-i-pare-i-brigades-se-nendeteseve-shqiptare/
15 'Me nëndetësen "105", notuam 22 ditë nën ujë si sfidë ndaj kërcënimit sovjetik e amerikan.' https://sot.com.al/dossier/me-n%C3%ABndet%C3%ABsen-%E2%80%9C105%E2%80%9D-notuam-22-dit%C3%AB-n%C3%ABn-uj%C3%AB-si-sfid%C3%AB-ndaj-k%C3%ABrc%C3%ABnimit-sovjetik-e-amerikan
16 Notably, there remains lots of confusion and unreliability in even the most authoritative Albanian sources. In his book *Submarine 105: Memoirs of a Commander*, Aleko Pojani claims that he commanded a submarine with a pennant number 105, including in the period 1959-1961, in the period of confrontation with Soviet sailors. However, an investigation by an Albanian newspaper, based on a letter from a reader, showed that at the time of the 'interception' of the boat from Soviet sailors, the commander of the boat was on the sick leave (and it was not Pojani) and the submarine was commanded by his deputy Beqir Gërbi. As for the pennant number of the submarine, 105 was the pennant number from the aforementioned propaganda film *Face to Face* of 1979, and the pennant number of the submarine in 1961 was 196. Thus, in the book of the most famous Albanian submariner, reality intersects with cinematic fantasies.

Chapter 2

1 'Подводничарят капитан II ранг Тодор Христов Георгиев (Големият Федя)' https://morskivestnik.com/compass/news/2019/032019/images/TodorGeorgievPL.pdf
2 'ПРЕДИ 60 ГОДИНИ – В БОЙНИЯ СТРОЙ НА БЪЛГАРСКИТЕ ВМС ПОСТЪПВАТ НА ВЪОРЪЖЕНИЕ ПОДВОДНИЦИ ОТ ПРОЕКТ 613.' https://morskivestnik.com/compass/news/2018/092018/images/Predi60g_12092018.pdf

Chapter 3

1 Александр Розин, 'Военно-морское сотрудничество СССР с ВМС Египта. Часть 1.' http://alerozin.narod.ru/EgyptNavySoviet1.htm
2 For intricate details on the famous 'Czechoslovak Arms Deal', see Smisek, *Czechoslovak Arms Exports to the Middle East*, Volume 3.
3 М. Саранчук, 'В ПОХОД С АРАБСКИМ ЭКИПАЖЕМ' http://www.vetsubmlat.narod.ru/vet111.html
4 А. Розин, 'Военно-морское сотрудничество СССР с ВМС Египта. Часть 2.' http://alerozin.narod.ru/EgyptNavySoviet2.htm
5 А.А.Бедеров., 'Международное военное сотрудничество' http://www.vetsubmlat.narod.ru/vet22.html
6 Ashraf Refaat, 'Naval aspects of the 1967 War', *Al-Ahram Weekly*, 7 May 2013,
7 А. Розин, 'Военно-морское сотрудничество СССР с ВМС Египта. Часть 3', *Alerozin.narod.ru*
8 Churchill et al, *The Six Day War*, p.94
9 URI BAR-JOSEPH, 'How An Egyptian Spy Stopped The Deadliest Terror Plot On Israel In History', Noema, 31 August 2016
10 Herzog, *War of Atonement*, pp.263-64.
11 O'Ballance, *No Victor, No Vanquished*, p.158

12 O'Ballance, *No Victor, No Vanquished*, p.153
13 https://group73historians.com/%D8%AD%D8%B1.../1694-19092023 - 'Exclusive: The role of Egyptian submarines in the October War in detail'
14 Rear Admiral Ashraf M. Refaat, 'How the Egyptian Navy Fought the October War', *Proceedings*, March 1995

Chapter 4

1 А. В. Попов, 'Экономика Индонезии: современное состояние и тенденции развития', Федеральное государственное бюджетное учреждение науки Институт востоковедения РАН Институт стран Востока, Москва, 2019
2 И.В.Безик 'Советско-индонезийское военно-морское сотрудничество', Советско-индонезийское военно-морское сотрудничество, 1999
3 'Perjalanan Rahasia ke Polandia', detik.com, 26 August 2017.
4 http://alerozin.narod.ru/IndonesiaSovietNavy1.htm
5 Лебедько В.Г., 'Верность долгу' Санкт-Петербург, 'Развитие', 2005 г.
6 http://alerozin.narod.ru/IndonesiaSovietNavy3.htm
7 https://military.wikireading.ru/hLQnXMeuSh
8 Sadly, it remains unknown exactly which of the Soviet Navy's vessels became which of the Indonesian Navy's vessels.
9 Notably, even before the Operation Jayawijaya, on 1 March 1962, the Indonesians initiated the Operations Antaredja and Imam Sura. These envisaged a power demonstration in the Morotai area, off the coast of West Irian (New Guinea), above and below 2° latitude, and lasted until mid-July 1962. In turn, these manoeuvres were a part of the Indonesian Operation Trikora, the aim of which was to seize and annex the Dutch overseas territory of New Guinea. Among the involved vessels of the Indonesian Navy was the submarine RI *Nanggala*.
10 https://intisari.grid.id/read/03208220/nekat-mendaratkan-pasukan-di-tengah-kepungan-kapal-perang-belanda-awak-kapal-selam-alri-akhirnya-mendapat-penghargaan-bintang-sakti?page=all
11 https://news.detik.com/x/detail/intermeso/20170826/Merebut-Papua-dari-Belanda/
12 https://www.globalsecurity.org/military/world/indonesia/kri-lst-teluk-langsa.htm
13 http://garudamiliter.blogspot.com/2012/02/kapal-selam-whiskey-class_17.html#
14 https://news.detik.com/x/detail/intermeso/20170826/Operasi-Rahasia-di-Perairan-Pakistan-/. Notably, an agreement about the demarcation of a mutual border between India and Indonesia was signed only 14 January 1977.
15 "Soviet Agrees to Extend Term of Indonesian Debt", The New York Times, 28 August 1970, Page 4, https://www.nytimes.com/1970/08/28/archives/soviet-agrees-to-extend-term-of-indonesian-debt.html
16 https://www.indonesiamandiri.web.id/2023/08/raden-pandji-poernomo-komandan-kapal.html
17 https://www.beritatrans.com/artikel/227648/Mengenal-Satuan-Khusus-Kapal-Selam-TNI-AL-Korps-Hiu-Kencana/
18 https://nationalinterest.org/blog/buzz/asias-submarine-powerhouse-you-might-not-know-about-53422
19 https://dewey.petra.ac.id/repository/jiunkpe/jiunkpe/s1/jdkv/2006/jiunkpe-ns-s1-2006-42402074-4249-monkasel-chapter2.pdf
20 https://manado.tribunnews.com/2020/05/20/gara-gara-sampah-made-in-indonesia-australia-ketar-ketir-seakan-tak-percaya-kapal-asing-bisa-masuk
21 http://weaponstechnology.blogspot.com/2011/07/kisah-kisah-kapal-selam-tni-al-50-tahun.html
22 https://www.goodnewsfromindonesia.id/2021/04/26/disegani-dunia-sejarah-kapal-selam-indonesia-yang-tabah-sampai-akhir
23 https://militermeter.com/kri-ri-alugoro-406-bukti-indonesia-pernah-uji-tembak-rudal-jelajah-dari-kapal-selam/
24 http://defense-studies.blogspot.com/2020/11/kisah-ketika-kapal-selam-indonesia-buat.html
25 https://www.merdeka.com/histori/kisah-lucu-amp-heroik-awak-kapal-selam-tni-al-buatan-uni-soviet-tabah-sampai-akhir.html

Chapter 5

1 'SS Romeo Class Project 13', https://www.globalsecurity.org/military/world/dprk/s-romeo.htm
2 Александр Розин, 'Советский флот и ВМС Северной Кореи (КНДР)' http://alerozin.narod.ru/KNDRiUSSR.htm

Chapter 7

1 https://www.baike.com/wikiid/9415945474186614492view_id=3ck1tjpqanw000
2 С. И. Титушкин, 'Подводные лодки 613 проекта' https://coollib.com/b/300925-sergey-ivanovich-titushkin-podvodnyie-lodki-613-proekta/read
3 https://zhuanlan.zhihu.com/p/455268751
4 https://archive.is/20120905012640/http://www.oklink.net/online/tougao/142058/283218.htm
5 https://naval-encyclopedia.com/cold-war/china/type-03-class-submarines.php
6 https://web.archive.org/web/20080522104052/http://60.250.180.26/pla/5741/5209.html
7 https://baike.baidu.hk/item/6603%E5%9E%8B%E5%B8%B8%E8%A6%8F%E5%8B%95%E5%8A%9B%E6%94%BB%E6%93%8A%E6%BD%9B%E8%89%87/1130145

Chapter 8

1 http://www.mdk2.lublin.pl/ORPOrzel/o_okrecie_2.html
2 https://web.archive.org/web/20091020053829/http://www.wolf.pl/okret_sokol.html
3 Henryk Sołkiewicz (red.): Ewolucyjny rozwój sił okrętowych Marynarki Wojennej w latach 1945–2010. Gdynia: Wydawnictwo BP/Akademia Marynarki Wojennej, 2015, s. 136.
4 Tadeusz Grzesikowski, Czesław Rudzki., 'ORP Kondor (294)', *Morza, Statki i Okręty*, N.3, 2000, p.25
5 Tadeusz Grzesikowski, Czesław Rudzki., 'ORP Kondor (294'), *Morza, Statki i Okręty*, N.3, 2000, p.27
6 Tadeusz Grzesikowski, Czesław Rudzki., 'ORP Kondor (294)', *Morza, Statki i Okręty*, N.4, 2000, p.34
7 Tadeusz Grzesikowski, Czesław Rudzki., 'ORP Kondor (294)', *Morza, Statki i Okręty*, N.4, 2000, p.39
8 https://bhmw.wp.mil.pl/pl/articles6-aktualnosci/zmarl-komandor-franciszek-wrobel-dowodca-okretu-hydrograficznego-orp-kopernik-w-latach-1971-1986-mial-89-lat/
9 https://archiwum.mw.wp.mil.pl/mw.mil.pl/indexe0cd.html?akcja=archiwum&years=2008&months=&id=18794

Chapter 9

1 http://alerozin.narod.ru/SyriaSub613.htm
2 https://group73historians.com/%D8%AD%D8%B1.../1694-19092023
3 'Грамоты от Министра Обороны Сирии' http://xn--b1atgapb.xn--p1ai/gramoty-ot-ministra-oborony-sirii/

ABOUT THE AUTHOR

Dmitry Zubkov from Russia, a banker with 25 years of experience, has a lifelong interest in the subject of military history and has written a number of books and articles in Russian on a variety of related subjects. His particular area of interest is the little-studied issue of Soviet arms export during the Cold War, especially warships. His studies involve little known details of the warships' careers, the warships' influence on the buildup of the recipient navies, and the experiences of their crews.